MW01687742

To

From

Date

An **Extraordinary** Life

...shaken together and running over

THE CORNERSTONE PUBLISHING

Joseph Olowe

An Extraordinary Life

...shaken together and running over

Paperback ISBN: 978-1-944652-65-4
eBook ISBN: 978-1-944652-68-5

Published by:
Cornerstone Publishing
A Division of Cornerstone Creativity Group LLC
Info@thecornerstonepublishers.com
www.thecornerstonepublishers.com

516.547.4999

Author's Contact

For booking to speak at your next event or to order bulk copies of this book please use information below:

P. O Box 10499
El Paso, TX 79995
1-800-561-9170 or +1 915-478-8807
www.drjosepholowe.com | info@drjosepholowe.com

DEDICATION

To my father in the Lord, Pastor Olubayo Akinrinola. You showed me the way of salvation and have been by my side all the way. Through thick and thin, you labored over me and instilled in me a second-to-none drive and encouragement to grow in my faith and devotion to my family.

I will forever be indebted to you for leading the way.

ACKNOWLEDGMENTS

I will like to appreciate my savior Jesus Christ from whom all blessings flow. My sincere gratitude to my wife and partner in ministry, Omolade for her relentless pursuit of excellence for our family first and ministry.

To my children Olamide, Simi and Dare who have given me an opportunity to practice what I am preaching.

To my ministry team, first to my able editor who I consider as a gift from heaven to me, Pastor Joseph Ola and to Daniel Emonido who I refer to as mighty Danny, for all the divine graphics; many thanks. To Pastor Gbenga Showunmi and his professional team at Cornerstone Publishing, thank you for making this dream come true.

To a good friend of mine, Pastor David Olayemi — the first man apart from my family, who sincerely believed in my writing gift and encouraged me to pursue my dream — may the God of heaven never forget your labor of love.

CONTENTS

Dedication.....5

Acknowledgments.....7

Introduction.....11

1. Anointing Breaks the Yoke.....17

2. Giving and the Gifts of the Spirit.....41

3. The Word: Rhema or Logos?.....51

4. Abounding in Wisdom.....61

5. The Power of Vision.....91

6. Follow Through With God.....113

7. Pride, Haughtiness And Humility.....125

8. High Praise And Worship.....147

About The Author.....163

INTRODUCTION

God's plan for the human race became evident after the creation of man. Like a man that wrote his will—an expression of how he wishes to share his properties after his demise—God gave a candid expression of His intent for the human race. After those six days of creation, He entered into His rest and has since designated man to continue with creation having being made in His image and likeness with the same inherent ability to create.

> *"And God blessed them, and God said unto them, Be fruitful, and multiply, and replenish the earth, and subdue it: and have dominion over the fish of the sea, and over the fowl of the air, and over every living thing that moveth upon the earth." (Genesis 1:28)*

What an extraordinary life God intended us to have! First and foremost, He wants us to be **FRUITFUL**, which means we are to bear more fruits as evidence of our existence in Him. Anything that is not bringing fruit is as good as dead.

"And the Lord shall make thee plenteous in goods, in the fruit of thy body, and in the fruit of thy cattle, and in the fruit of thy ground, in the land which the Lord sware unto thy fathers to give thee." (Deuteronomy 28:11)

Besides, He wants us to **MULTIPLY** at an exponential increase in all areas of our lives. No wonder God said one will chase a thousand and two will put ten thousand to flight.

"The Lord shall open unto thee his good treasure, the heaven to give the rain unto thy land in his season, and to bless all the work of thine hand: and thou shalt lend unto many nations, and thou shalt not borrow." (Deuteronomy 28:12)

Then He wants us to **REPLENISH** the earth. This means to reproduce what was already done. So what was it that God did with the earth that we are to replicate? God restored order to a chaotic universe and we as the people of God need to continue doing that.

There are scriptures that tell us how to bring order in our everyday life as we yield to His leading. With our steps been ordered by the Lord, everything that is in us and around us will automatically become orderly.

"The steps of a good man are ordered by the Lord: and he delighteth in his way." (Psalm 37:23)

God also intends for us to **SUBDUE** the earth. God has made us royal priests and we are seated with Him in the heavenly places and from there we have everything under our feet, because the earth is His footstool. We are heavily protected.

"The Lord said unto my Lord, Sit thou at my right hand, until I make thine enemies thy footstool." (Psalm 110:1)

"He suffered no man to do them wrong: yea, he reproved kings for their sakes; Saying, Touch not mine anointed, and do my prophets no harm." (Psalm 105:14-15)

And ultimately, God wants us to **HAVE DOMINION**. with this index of His blessing over the human race, God made us the keeper of His creation. Adam was the keeper of His garden and when he lost that dominion, God Himself made a way through Jesus to reestablish it.

"Knowing that Christ being raised from the dead dieth no more; death hath no more dominion over him. For sin shall not have dominion over you: for ye are not under the law, but under grace." (Romans 6:9)

Grace is what God provided us with—all these blessings which we received. Check this out:

- In the Old Testament

"And it shall come to pass, if thou shalt hearken diligently unto the voice of the Lord thy God, to observe and to do all his commandments which I command thee this day, that the Lord thy God will set thee on high above all nations of the earth: And all these blessings shall come on thee, and overtake thee, if thou shalt hearken unto the voice of the Lord thy God. Blessed shalt thou be in the city, and blessed shalt thou be in the field. Blessed shall be the fruit of thy body, and the fruit of thy ground, and the fruit of thy cattle, the increase of thy kine, and the flocks of thy sheep. Blessed shall be thy basket and

thy store. Blessed shalt thou be when thou comest in, and blessed shalt thou be when thou goest out. The Lord shall cause thine enemies that rise up against thee to be smitten before thy face: they shall come out against thee one way, and flee before thee seven ways. The Lord shall command the blessing upon thee in thy storehouses, and in all that thou settest thine hand unto; and he shall bless thee in the land which the Lord thy God giveth thee. The Lord shall establish thee and holy people unto himself, as he hath sworn unto thee, if thou shalt keep the commandments of the Lord thy God, and walk in his ways. And all people of the earth shall see that thou art called by the name of the Lord; and they shall be afraid of thee. And the Lord shall make thee plenteous in goods, in the fruit of thy body, and in the fruit of thy cattle, and in the fruit of thy ground, in the land which the Lord sware unto thy fathers to give thee. The Lord shall open unto thee his good treasure, the heaven to give the rain unto thy land in his season, and to bless all the work of thine hand: and thou shalt lend unto many nations, and thou shalt not borrow. And the Lord shall make thee the head, and not the tail; and thou shalt be above only, and thou shalt not be beneath; if that thou hearken unto the commandments of the Lord thy God, which I command thee this day, to observe and to do them:" (Deuteronomy 28:1-13)

- In the New Testament

"The thief cometh not, but for to steal, and to kill, and to destroy: I am come that they might have life, and that they might have it more abundantly." (John 10:10)

As believers, we have access to SUPER ABUNDANCE

and are meant to lead an EXTRAORDINARY LIFE. The question is how can we lead this extraordinary life? To make a very good steak, we need the right seasoning for it to be tasty. Likewise, there are some ingredients that must be present in one's life for such to become an EXTRAORDINARY LIFE. Let us journey together to discover these ingredients that will undoubtedly transform our lives into EXTRAORDINARY and SUPER ABUNDANT lives.

CHAPTER 1

ANOINTING BREAKS THE YOKE

"But there is a spirit in man: and the inspiration of the Almighty giveth them understanding." (Job 32:8)

There is a spirit in every man; in fact, man is essentially a spirit that has a soul and dwells in a body. But for every believer, upon their salvation, the "inspiration of the Almighty"—the Holy Spirit that the Father sent after Jesus ascended on high—comes with the unction that we need in order to live a life that is overflowing. The Holy Spirit does this by releasing upon us an anointing to breakthrough.

"And it shall come to pass in that day, that his burden shall be taken away from off thy shoulder, and his yoke from off thy neck, and the yoke shall be destroyed because of the anointing." (Isaiah 10:27)

One of the verses of the famous Psalms 23 highlights the fact that it is the anointing that makes our cup to run over and our horn to be exalted high like that of a unicorn.

"Thou preparest a table before me in the presence of mine

enemies: thou anointest my head with oil; my cup runneth over." (Psalm 23:5)

"But my horn shalt thou exalt like the horn of an unicorn: I shall be anointed with fresh oil. Mine eye also shall see my desire on mine enemies, an mine ears shall hear my desire of the wicked that rise up against me. The righteous shall flourish like the palm tree: he shall grow like a cedar in Lebanon." (Psalms 92:10-12)

There are few questions we need to provide answers for in order to understand the role of the anointing in birthing an extraordinary life. Here are some of the questions.

- What is the purpose of anointing?
- What are the functions of anointing?
- Where does anointing come from?
- Who gets anointed?
- How do you get anointed?
- What gets anointed?
- When do you get anointed?

"The Spirit of the Lord is upon me, because he hath anointed me to preach the gospel to the poor; he hath sent me to heal the brokenhearted, to preach deliverance to the captives, and recovering of sight to the blind, to set at liberty them that are bruised, To preach the acceptable year of the Lord." (Luke 4:18-19)

"He suffered no man to do them wrong: yea, he reproved kings for their sakes; Saying, Touch not mine anointed, and do my prophets no harm." (Psalms 105:14-15)

WHAT IS THE PURPOSE OF ANOINTING?

When we think about anointing, we tend to think about breakthrough or people falling when hands are laid on them, but let us trace anointing to the beginning of creation. In the beginning, the earth was without form, void and darkness was everywhere. The spirit of The Lord moved and God said "let there be LIGHT". Everything God created began to fall in place because the light of God brought illumination. **The main purpose of anointing is to bring illumination to our life and situation.**

> *"And God said, Let there be light: and there was light." (Genesis 1:3)*

God said let there be light, and there was light. The source of an extraordinary life is Jesus Christ, Who is the light of the world. Jesus Christ (and 'Christ' means 'the Anointed One with His Anointing) came into action when God said let there be light.

> *"All things were made by him; and without him was not anything made that was made. In him was life; and the life was the light of men." (John 1:3-4)*

All things were made by Him, means that all creation from the beginning were made by Him (Jesus Christ). The anointing creates things; anything that you are desiring has to come from the 'Father of Light' or 'the anointing'.

WHAT ARE THE FUNCTIONS OF ANOINTING?

Let us look at this scripture closely:

> *"The Spirit of the Lord is upon me, because he hath anointed me to preach the gospel to the poor; he hath sent me to heal the brokenhearted, to preach deliverance to the captives, and recovering of sight to the blind, to set at liberty them that are bruised, To preach the acceptable year of the Lord." (Luke 4:18-19)*

Here is Jesus making a statement about the principal functions of the anointing; that same Spirit that moved upon the deep in the beginning was upon Jesus in this text and the functions of the same were stated, viz:

1. To preach the gospel to the poor.

The anointing we seek is to preach the gospel to the poor. What do we tell the people about Jesus? It is very simple, God said 'let there be light and there was light'; this is the same good news we are to preach! This assignment of preaching the good news is the true evidence of an extraordinary life. Why? When you have something good that can benefit other people, you want to share it with people far and near. Let us look at what Jesus said about the light.

> *"Then spake Jesus again unto them, saying, I am the light of the world: he that followeth me shall not walk in darkness, but shall have the light of life." (John 8:12)*

> *"But all things that are reproved are made manifest by the light: for whatsoever doth make manifest is light." (Ephesians 5:13)*

What better news can we share about Jesus, than letting the world know that He is the real light? To make it in life, we need to have the light of life. When people embrace walking in the light of God, then the desire to do evil will disappear.

> *"As long as I am in the world, I am the light of the world." (John 9:5)*

> *"I am come a light into the world, that whosoever believeth on me should not abide in darkness." (John 12:46)*

As long as we are in the world, then His light MUST continue to shine. There is enough darkness in the world, and so it becomes our responsibility by the empowerment of His anointing to share with the people that WHOSOEVER believes on Jesus will not abide in darkness.

Will you do that today? Will you share this good news with two or three people today? As you do so, His anointing will find even greater expression in your life.

Food for thought:

> *"For with thee is the fountain of life: in thy light shall we see light." (Psalms 36:9)*

When other people see the light in you, you become an epistle that people read. Be the light of the world and you will see His anointing breaking yokes.

> *"But if we walk in the light, as he is in the light, we have fellowship one with another, and the blood of Jesus Christ his Son cleanseth us from all sin." (1 John 1:7)*

"For ye were sometimes darkness, but now are ye light in the Lord: walk as children of light" (Ephesians 5:8)

"But all things that are reproved are made manifest by the light: for whatsoever doth make manifest is light." (Ephesians 5:13)

2. To preach deliverance to the captives.

Jesus is the only one that can turn your captivity around—not any man, prayer apprentice nor deliverance minister (as they are called).

"When the Lord turned again the captivity of Zion, we were like them that dream." (Psalms 126:1)

To preach deliverance is to point people back to Jesus, and when Jesus delivers these people, that same anointing will create an extraordinary life for you. You are a carrier of Jesus—a representative of Christ with the full benefits and privileges attached to that divine 'diplomatic responsibility' of being an ambassador of Christ. Solomon set a good example of preaching deliverance to the people of God when he built a temple for the Lord:

"If they sin against thee, (for there is no man which sinneth not,) and thou be angry with them, and deliver them over before their enemies, and they carry them away captives unto a land far off or near; Yet if they bethink themselves in the land whither they are carried captive, and turn and pray unto thee in the land of their captivity, saying, We have sinned, we have done amiss, and have dealt wickedly; If they return to thee with all their heart and with all their soul in the land of their captivity, whither they have carried them captives, and pray toward their land, which thou gavest unto their

fathers, and toward the city which thou hast chosen, and toward the house which I have built for thy name: Then hear thou from the heavens, even from thy dwelling place, their prayer and their supplications, and maintain their cause, and forgive thy people which have sinned against thee." (2 Chronicles 6:36-39)

The essence of this prayer is to show us that we need to point people back to God for their complete deliverance.

Digging deeper into this, there is an allusion.

"And God said, Let the waters under the heaven be gathered together unto one place, and let the dry land appear: and it was so." (Genesis 1:9)

God created the land on the third day when He called the earth out of the dust. The Lord brought forth man from this same dust and breathed into his nostril the breath of life.

It is not a coincidence that Jesus resurrected on the third day; He was able to lead captivity captive and delivered gifts unto men because He was able deal with anything underneath the earth and in the heavens that could hold us captive.

"Wherefore he saith, When he ascended up on high, he led captivity captive, and gave gifts unto men. (Now that he ascended, what is it but that he also descended first into the lower parts of the earth? He that descended is the same also that ascended up far above all heavens, that he might fill all things.)" (Ephesians 4:8-10)

"That he might fill all things" what a phrase! What do you need to overflow? Jesus can and will fill all things for you, till you overflow.

Food for thought:

> *"Shall the prey be taken from the mighty, or the lawful captive delivered? But thus saith the Lord, Even the captives of the mighty shall be taken away, and the prey of the terrible shall be delivered: for I will contend with him that contendeth with thee, and I will save thy children." (Isaiah 49:24-25)*

It does not matter how you became a captive, The Lord will turn it around for you whatever it is, be it financial, barrenness, sickness and any form of addiction.

3. To preach the acceptable year of The Lord.
To fully understand this, we need to look at the meaning of the word **acceptable.**

It simply means **pleasing to the receiver, satisfactory, agreeable and welcoming**. It also means **meeting the minimum requirements**. Knowing the meaning of that word—acceptable—gives us a good insight into what 'the acceptable year of The Lord' is all about. It started about 2000 years ago.

> *"Knowing this first, that no prophecy of the scripture is of any private interpretation." (2 Peter 1:20)*

The word of God interprets itself. The acceptable year of The Lord is the year Jesus Christ was crucified and resurrected. From that time on, everyone of us that accepted Jesus as our personal Savior became accepted into the beloved by the minimum requirement of confessing and accepting Jesus as our Lord and Savior. What a good news and the very beginning of an overflowing and extraordinary life.

Paul the apostle of the New Testament made a bold declaration:

> *"This is a faithful saying, and worthy of all acceptation, that Christ Jesus came into the world to save sinners; of whom I am chief." (1 Timothy 1:15)*

Peter also made the same declaration about who is accepted in the acceptable year of The Lord:

> *"Then Peter opened his mouth, and said, Of a truth I perceive that God is no respecter of persons: But in every nation he that feareth him, and worketh righteousness, is accepted with him." (Acts 10:34, 35)*

This is the beginning of an overflowing life. If we desire to live that life then we must share the news about the acceptable year of The Lord.

> *"For the kingdom of God is not meat and drink; but righteousness, and peace, and joy in the Holy Ghost. For him that in these things serveth Christ is acceptable to God, and approved of men." (Romans 14:17-18)*

Do you need an overflow of righteousness (right standing with God), or peace and joy? The Holy Spirit will help you to be acceptable to God and also approved of men.

Food for thought:

> *"I beseech you therefore, brethren, by the mercies of God, that ye present your bodies a living sacrifice, holy, acceptable unto God, which is your reasonable service. And be not conformed to this world: but be ye transformed by the renewing of your mind, that ye may prove what is that good, and acceptable, and perfect, will of God." (Romans 12:1-2)*

A good, acceptable and perfect will of God leads to an overflowing life. Let us share the good news.

What does it mean to be accepted in the beloved?

> *"Grace be to you, and peace, from God our Father, and from the Lord Jesus Christ. Blessed be the God and Father of our Lord Jesus Christ, who hath blessed us with all spiritual blessings in heavenly places in Christ: According as he hath chosen us in him before the foundation of the world, that we should be holy and without blame before him in love: Having predestined us unto the adoption of children by Jesus Christ to himself, according to the good pleasure of his will, To the praise of the glory of his grace, wherein he hath made us accepted in the beloved. In whom we have redemption through his blood, the forgiveness of sins, according to the riches of his grace; wherein he hath abounded toward us in all wisdom and prudence;" (Ephesians 1:2-8)*

In the acceptable year of the Lord, we have come into covenant with Him for an overflowing life and we have been accepted in the beloved through the following:

- He has blessed us with all spiritual blessings in the heavenly places.
- We have been chosen before the foundation of the world.
- We came in by adoption through Jesus Christ.
- He has made us accepted into the beloved.
- We have redemption through his blood, the forgiveness of sins.
- We are abounding in all wisdom and prudence.

Paul gave us a list of prayer points so that we can enjoy

the fullness of this overflowing and extraordinary life, let us look at the prayer:

> *"I cease not to give thanks for you, making mention of you in my prayers; That the God of our Lord Jesus Christ, the Father of glory, may give unto you the spirit of wisdom and revelation in the knowledge of him: The eyes of your understanding being enlightened; that ye may know what is the hope of his calling, and what the riches of the glory of his inheritance in the saints, And what is the exceeding greatness of his power to us-ward who believe, according to the working of his mighty power, Which he wrought in Christ, when he raised him from the dead, and set him at his own right hand in the heavenly places, Far above all principality, and power, and might, and dominion, and every name that is named, not only in this world, but also in that which is to come: And hath put all things under his feet, and gave him to be the head over all things to the church, Which is his body, the fullness of him that filleth all in all." (Ephesians 1:16-23)*

Let us pray this together as you continue to read this book.

1. That The Lord will give us the spirit of wisdom and revelation in the knowledge of him.
2. That the eyes of our understanding be enlightened.
3. That we may know the hope of His calling.
4. That we may know the riches of the glory of His inheritance in us.
5. That we may know the exceeding greatness of His power towards us, over all principality and power here now and in the world to come.
6. That we may know that all things are under His feet.

How can we go wrong? We are destined to live an overflowing and extraordinary life. I challenge you to pray this prayer for next seven days and watch what the Lord shall do in your life.

Food for thought:

> *"We then, as workers together with him, beseech you also that ye receive not the grace of God in vain. (For he saith, I have heard thee in a time accepted, and in the day of salvation have I succoured thee: behold, now is the accepted time; behold, now is the day of salvation.) Giving no offence in any thing, that the ministry be not blamed:" (2 Corinthians 6:1-3)*

We are workers together with him, He is going to hear us because this is the accepted time in the acceptable year of the Lord.

We have examined what we need to preach about for us to have an overflowing and extraordinary life as result of fulfilling the actual purpose for a life that is anointed. An extraordinary life is anointed to demonstrate faith by meeting practical needs, putting action behind their faith.

> *"Yea, a man may say, Thou hast faith, and I have works: shew me thy faith without thy works, and I will shew thee my faith by my works." (James 2:18)*

To fulfill the actual purpose of the anointing, there are three action words that The Lord will draw our attentions to.

- He has SENT me to heal the brokenhearted
- RECOVERING of sight to the blind
- To SET at liberty them that are bruised.

1. He has SENT me to heal the brokenhearted: We have been SENT to heal the brokenhearted. To be brokenhearted is to be burdened with great sorrow, grief, and disappointment. So how do we heal the brokenhearted?

> *"Blessed be God, even the Father of our Lord Jesus Christ, the Father of mercies, and the God of all comfort; Who comforteth us in all our tribulation, that we may be able to comfort them which are in any trouble, by the comfort wherewith we ourselves are comforted of God." (2 Corinthians 1:3-4)*

From this scripture we see that whatever is it that you are going through or have gone through is a point of reference to comfort the people around us the way we have received our comfort from God. No wonder Apostle Paul was able to write two-thirds of the New Testament.

> *"Who shall separate us from the love of Christ? Shall tribulation, or distress, or persecution, or famine, or nakedness, or peril, or sword? As it is written, for thy sake we are killed all the day long; we are accounted as sheep for the slaughter. Nay, in all these things we are more than conquerors through him that loved us. For I am persuaded, that neither death, nor life, nor angels, nor principalities, nor powers, nor things present, nor things to come, nor height, nor depth, nor any other creature, shall be able to separate us from the love of God, which is in Christ Jesus our Lord." (Romans 8:35-39)*

This understanding helped Paul to comfort us with same comfort he was comforted by God. In like manner, WE ARE SENT, therefore, LET US GO. The signs that follow believers follow those that obey the great commission to "go". When we "go", we will begin to see the anointing working in its fullness in our lives and we will begin to enjoy the overflowing and extraordinary life created by the anointing.

Food for thought:

> *"As thou hast sent me into the world, even so have I also sent them into the world." (John 17:18)*

We have a marching order from the Commander: the field is ripe for a great harvest. Jesus was able to give us comfort from what He survived:

> *"He is despised and rejected of men; a man of sorrows, and acquainted with grief: and we hid as it were our faces from him; he was despised, and we esteemed him not. Surely he hath borne our griefs, and carried our sorrows: yet we did esteem him stricken, smitten of God, and afflicted. But he was wounded for our transgressions, he was bruised for our iniquities: the chastisement of our peace was upon him; and with his stripes we are healed." (Isaiah 53:3-5)*

Jesus was despised and rejected for us to be accepted and healed, How far are you willing to go to heal the brokenhearted? Truth is that it's not going to be easy. When you are sent, there might be some level of discomfort that comes with doing that which He commanded. You could be misunderstood or misinterpreted, but it doesn't matter. Nothing changes the fact that you have been sent to go and comfort the brokenhearted.

2. Recovering of sight to the blind:

This is an interesting concept which comes with our calling. Not only have we been sent to heal the brokenhearted; we have also been sent to facilitate the recovery of sight to the blind. To recover is:

to get back or regain, to make up for or make good (simple English definition)

- To obtain by judgement in a court of law or to recover damages from wrong (Judicially)
- To gain or regain possession of a fumble (in American football)
- It is very important to see the word "recover" from these three angles so as to get an in-depth analysis of this simple but powerful word.

"And these signs shall follow them that believe; In my name shall they cast out devils; they shall speak with new tongues; They shall take up serpents; and if they drink any deadly thing, it shall not hurt them; they shall lay hands on the sick, and they shall recover." (Mark 16:17-18)

It takes the anointing to bring about a recovery of lost benefits, but before a recovery can take place, it involves a level of action on our part. We must actively engage in telling people about the power of recovery found in Jesus Christ. The fact that Jesus in his earthly ministry recovered the sight of a good number of blind people has some profound spiritual implications regarding sight. It takes a recovered sight to discover the hidden secrets that will unlock our abundant life.

"The secret of the Lord is with them that fear him; and he will shew them his covenant." (Psalms 25:14)

"The secret things belong unto the Lord our God: but those things which are revealed belong unto us and to

> *our children forever, that we may do all the words of this law." (Deuteronomy 29:29)*

Food for thought:

> *"He that dwelleth in the secret place of the most High shall abide under the shadow of the Almighty." (Psalms 91:1)*

Secret things are discovered in secret places. What do we need to get back or regain? To make up for or make good? If blindness is the problem, what are we blinded to? To live an extraordinary life we must have access to God's treasures. When Adam and Eve sinned at the beginning, they lost that access; but thanks be to God for the second Adam (Jesus Christ) Who has reopened the treasury and given us access. Jesus fulfilled the judicial obligation on the cross because he has paid for our full recovery. He said, "it is finished" on the cross; nothing can be added or taken away. Now we have recovered the blunder ball by Adam and Eve; what an extraordinary life we can live now. Praise God!

> *"The Lord shall open unto thee his good treasure, the heaven to give the rain unto thy land in his season, and to bless all the work of thine hand: and thou shalt lend unto many nations, and thou shalt not borrow." (Deuteronomy 28:12)*

> *"And I will give thee the treasures of darkness, and hidden riches of secret places, that thou mayest know that I, the Lord, which call thee by thy name, am the God of Israel." (Isaiah 45:3)*

Food for thought:

"But upon mount Zion shall be deliverance, and there shall be holiness; and the house of Jacob shall possess their possessions. And the house of Jacob shall be a fire, and the house of Joseph a flame, and the house of Esau for stubble, and they shall kindle in them, and devour them; and there shall not be any remaining of the house of Esau; for the Lord hath spoken it." (Obadiah 1:17, 18)

3. To set at liberty them that are bruised:

Liberty is:

- Freedom from external or foreign rule; independence.
- Freedom from control, interference, obligation, restriction, hampering conditions; power or right of doing, thinking, speaking, according to choice.
- Freedom from captivity, confinement, or physical restraint: The prisoner soon regained his liberty. (thefreedictionary.com)

An extraordinary life is a liberated life. Jesus has secured our freedom spiritually from the place of the skull—and when we have liberty in our spirit, then we have liberty in every areas of our life.

"Stand fast therefore in the liberty wherewith Christ hath made us free, and be not entangled again with the yoke of bondage." (Galatians 5:1)

"Now the Lord is that Spirit: and where the Spirit of the Lord is, there is liberty." (2 Corinthians 3:17)

This, Jesus did again and again as an example for us to follow:

"Then Jesus went thence, and departed into the coasts of Tyre and Sidon. And, behold, a woman of Canaan came out of the same coasts, and cried unto him, saying, Have mercy on me, O Lord, thou Son of David; my daughter is grievously vexed with a devil. But he answered her not a word. And his disciples came and besought him, saying, Send her away; for she crieth after us. But he answered and said, I am not sent but unto the lost sheep of the house of Israel. Then came she and worshipped him, saying, Lord, help me. But he answered and said, It is not meet to take the children's bread, and to cast it to dogs. And she said, Truth, Lord: yet the dogs eat of the crumbs which fall from their masters' table. Then Jesus answered and said unto her, O woman, great is thy faith: be it unto thee even as thou wilt. And her daughter was made whole from that very hour." (Matthew 15:21-28)

There are a lot of unbelievers out there just waiting for us to engage them and bring the words of comfort and deliverance to them. Because of Jesus's sacrifice everyone is qualified to enjoy this liberty. As we have been sent, may we be available to play our part in their recovery and liberty.

WHERE DOES ANOINTING COME FROM?

The simple answer is that anointing comes from God. In fact, He has given each of us a measure of the anointing; it can only take God's anointing for us—mere dust—to talk, eat and do every other thing that we are able to do. We definitely owe God more than we think.

"And the Lord God formed man of the dust of the ground, and breathed into his nostrils the breath of life; and man became a living soul." (Genesis 2:7)

"The Spirit of God hath made me, and the breath of the Almighty hath given me life." (Job 33:4)

From the beginning, God's intention was to abide in us perpetually but the plan was aborted by man's disobedience. As we will see later in the scriptures, the template He used above for the release of His anointing upon us in the beginning became the same template used in fixing the issue of His indwelling anointing.

"And when he had said this, he breathed on them, and saith unto them, Receive ye the Holy Ghost:" (John 20:22)

From the time of Adam till Jesus appeared on the scene, God has been looking for a way to anoint us for great exploits. From Aaron to the prophets, the spirit of God came upon people usually after being anointed with oil and their lives never remained the same.

"Then went Samson down, and his father and his mother, to Timnath, and came to the vineyards of Timnath: and, behold, a young lion roared against him. And the Spirit of the Lord came mightily upon him, and he rent him as he would have rent a kid, and he had nothing in his hand: but he told not his father or his mother what he had done." (Judges 14:5-6)

"Then all the Midianites and the Amalekites and the children of the east were gathered together, and went over, and pitched in the valley of Jezreel. But the Spirit

of the Lord came upon Gideon, and he blew a trumpet; and Abi–ezer was gathered after him." (Judges 6:33-34)

"Then Samuel took a vial of oil, and poured it upon his head, and kissed him, and said, Is it not because the Lord hath anointed thee to be captain over his inheritance? And the Spirit of the Lord will come upon thee, and thou shalt prophesy with them, and shalt be turned into another man. And let it be, when these signs are come unto thee, that thou do as occasion serve thee; for God is with thee." (1 Samuel 10:1,6-7)

"Then the Spirit of the Lord came upon Jephthah, and he passed over Gilead, and Manasseh, and passed over Mizpeh of Gilead, and from Mizpeh of Gilead he passed over unto the children of Ammon." (Judges 11:29)

"And he poured of the anointing oil upon Aaron's head, and anointed him, to sanctify him." (Leviticus 8:12)

But the limitation that came with this type of anointing system is that the spirit or the anointing departs from the carrier as soon as the purpose for the anointing is accomplished. But God presented a perfect solution through Jesus Christ. Jesus paved the way for the indwelling Spirit that guides us from within to this abundant and overflowing life.

"And John bare record, saying, I saw the Spirit descending from heaven like a dove, and it abode upon him. And I knew him not: but he that sent me to baptize with water, the same said unto me, upon whom thou shalt see the Spirit descending, and remaining on him, the same is he which baptizeth with the Holy Ghost." (John 1:32-33)

Now we know that the true anointing comes from the father of light, and it abides and remains upon us.

Food for thought:

> *"How God anointed Jesus of Nazareth with the Holy Ghost and with power: who went about doing good, and healing all that were oppressed of the devil; for God was with him." (Acts 10:38)*

The anointing from above will bring down the hand of God as seen in the story of Obed of Edom.

HOW DO WE GET ANOINTED?

We have seen so far that God uses various method to anoint His people—He could breathe upon His chosen ones to release an unction upon them; when the prophets of old give a word of prophecy, the spirit or the anointing comes upon them; sometimes oil is poured upon His chosen ones and something supernatural happens—and God still uses all these methods today.

> *"Jesus Christ the same yesterday, and today, and forever." (Hebrews 13:8)*

WHO GETS ANOINTED?

In the Old Testament not everybody gets anointed; just priests, prophets, judges and kings. Whoever is not in any of these categories is out of luck and might not be used by God for any purpose. Thankfully in the new dispensation, Jesus has made all of us born again accepted in the beloved.

"And from Jesus Christ, who is the faithful witness, and the first begotten of the dead, and the prince of the kings of the earth. Unto him that loved us, and washed us from our sins in his own blood, And hath made us kings and priests unto God and his Father; to him be glory and dominion for ever and ever. Amen." (Revelation 1:5-6)

"And hast made us unto our God kings and priests: and we shall reign on the earth." (Revelation 5:10)

Therefore, we are anointed already for exploits.

"But the people that do know their God shall be strong, and do exploits." (Daniel 11:32b)

WHEN DO WE GET ANOINTED?

In the Old Testament people get anointed for a special occasion, special assignment, and special position. But in the New Testament, when you accept what Jesus has done for you, you automatically receive this anointing for exploits. But now, it is up to you to develop it and do mighty works for the Lord. The most powerful and anointed man or woman of God you know received the same measure of anointing at his or her new birth as you received, the difference is in their personal development of the anointing. How do we develop it? By constant prayers, fasting, worship and speaking in tongues.

WHAT GETS ANOINTED?

As controversial as this bit of the subject of anointing has become in the body of Christ today, I personally believe that you can anoint anything that God tells you to anoint because you are not answerable to anybody but to Him. Let's look at some strange things that got anointed in the Bible:

1. Balaam's Donkey

"And the Lord opened the mouth of the ass, and she said unto Balaam, What have I done unto thee, that thou hast smitten me these three times?" (Numbers 22:28)

2. Elijah's Mantle

"And it came to pass, when they were gone over, that Elijah said unto Elisha, Ask what I shall do for thee, before I be taken away from thee. And Elisha said, I pray thee, let a double portion of thy spirit be upon me." (2 Kings 2:9)

"And he took the mantle of Elijah that fell from him, and smote the waters, and said, where is the Lord God of Elijah? And when he also had smitten the waters, they parted hither and thither: and Elisha went over." (2 Kings 2:14)

3. The Ark of Covenant

God put His anointing on this wooden box so that it provides direction for His people.

"There was nothing in the ark save the two tables which Moses put therein at Horeb, when the Lord made a covenant with the children of Israel, when they came out of Egypt." (2 Chronicles 5:10)

God is God all by himself and He is not answerable to

you or to me. As for me and my house, we anoint the living and non-living things in our abode according to His direction and leading.

Food for thought:

> *"Where is the wise? Where is the scribe? Where is the disputer of this world? Hath not God made foolish the wisdom of this world? Because the foolishness of God is wiser than men; and the weakness of God is stronger than men." (1 Corinthians 1:20, 25)*

CHAPTER 2

GIVING AND THE GIFTS OF THE SPIRIT

"Give, and it shall be given unto you; good measure, pressed down, and shaken together, and running over, shall men give into your bosom. For with the same measure that ye mete withal it shall be measured to you again." (Luke 6:38)

GIVING

Jesus is not having a conversation here or asking for our opinion, it was a command given to us and He expects us to obey. The kingdom of God is not democratic; the Godhead rule by decree, and we are to obey.

In Luke 6:38 quoted above, Jesus highlights the benefits of what GIVING does to the giver. Among these many benefits, the one that stands out to me is the RUNNING OVER factor. 'Running over' happens when the container is full and there is no room for more, hence, the content begins to overflow down the side of the container. This kind of overflowing experience is not as a result of a one-time giving, NO. In fact, the extent of your running over experience depends on so many factors—the size of your container (for the same measure that ye mete withal it shall be measure to you again), the size of your obedience to the command of your giving, and so on.

You have a RUNNING OVER experience when you provide yourself a container that does not wax old so that there is no leakage. When you hand your container over to God, it cannot be stolen—no break-ins; only breakthroughs—and it will not fail to yield returns. Besides, no Ponzi scheme.

This comes with a good number of benefits:

- God will pay attention to your giving, and when He remembers your offerings, goodness happens.
- He will grant you your desires.
- Your walk and work will continually be under open heavens.

> *"Sell that ye have, and give alms; provide yourselves bags which wax not old, a treasure in the heavens that faileth not, where no thief approacheth, neither moth corrupteth. For where your treasure is, there will your heart be also." (Luke 12:33-34)*

> *"Lay not up for yourselves treasures upon earth, where moth and rust doth corrupt, and where thieves break through and steal: But lay up for yourselves treasures in heaven, where neither moth nor rust doth corrupt, and where thieves do not break through nor steal: For where your treasure is, there will your heart be also." (Matthew 6:19-21)*

> *"Remember all thy offerings, and accept thy burnt sacrifice; Selah. Grant thee according to thine own heart, and fulfil all thy counsel." (Psalms 20:3-4)*

> *"Bring ye all the tithes into the storehouse, that there may be meat in mine house, and prove me now herewith, saith the Lord of hosts, if I will not open you the windows of heaven, and pour you out a blessing, that there shall not be room enough to receive it. And I will rebuke the devourer for your sakes, and he shall not destroy the fruits of your ground; neither shall your vine cast her fruit before the time in the field, saith the Lord of hosts. And all nations shall call you blessed: for ye shall be a delightsome land, saith the Lord of hosts." (Malachi 3:10-12)*

David was a solid giver who led a great life despite all that went wrong with him—he was regarded as a man after God's own heart

Food for thought:

> *"He that observeth the wind shall not sow; and he that regardeth the clouds shall not reap." (Ecclesiastes 11:4)*

What is your situation or condition as we speak? Nothing should prevent you from giving. No matter how grim your situation might look like, if you are a giver do not regard the cloud because the harvest is certain. When you become a giver, your life becomes super charged and extraordinary.

Praise God who has abundance on His mind from the beginning of His relationship with us. From John 10: 10 we see that God has an idea of what kind of life He wants for us—an OVERFLOWING LIFE.

"The thief cometh not, but for to steal, and to kill, and to destroy: I am come that they might have life, and that they might have it more abundantly." (John 10:10)

GIFTS

The greatest gift from God to us is the gift of salvation. It is quite evident that God had an overflowing kingdom in mind when He set up the plan for Jesus to demonstrate His gift of obedience by going to the cross for us.

"Though he were a Son, yet learned he obedience by the things which he suffered; And being made perfect, he became the author of eternal salvation unto all them that obey him;" (Hebrews 5:8-9)

"And being found in fashion as a man, he humbled himself, and became obedient unto death, even the death of the cross." (Philippians 2:8)

But before any gift or gifting can become operational in the life of a believer, he/she must first receive the gift of salvation; it is only then that spiritual gifts can manifest.

Where does our gift come from?

Not all gifts finding expression in people's lives are gifts from God. That is why He expects us to judge all spirits. As true believers, our gifts—the kind that lead to an abundant and extraordinary life—all come from Him.

"Every good gift and every perfect gift is from above, and cometh down from the Father of lights, with whom is no variableness, neither shadow of turning." (James 1:17)

> *"Wherefore he saith, When he ascended up on high, he led captivity captive, and gave gifts unto men." (Ephesians 4:8)*

What are we supposed to do with our gift?
God does expect some things from us, having gifted us. We'll highlight some of them below:

1) *"But the manifestation of the Spirit is given to every man to profit withal." (1 Corinthians 12:7)* God expects us to profit from whatever gift that we are endowed with, so we can say that the purpose of a gift to the benefactor is to live an overflowing and extraordinary life.

2) *"A man's gift maketh room for him, and bringeth him before great men." (Proverbs 18:16)* Your gift should make room for you. You can make something out of nothing using your gift wisely. Your gift will also create an access to places regarded off limit for commoners. It will make you to sit in high places.

> *"He raiseth up the poor out of the dust, and lifteth up the beggar from the dunghill, to set them among princes, and to make them inherit the throne of glory: for the pillars of the earth are the Lord's, and he hath set the world upon them." (1 Samuel 2:8)*

I have thought about this Bible verse many times and I believe one of the ways this scripture can be fulfilled is through the gift that He endowed us with to make profit. This readily brings the story of both Joseph and David to mind. Joseph's gift brought him to the palace, and David's gift amongst other things helped him bring Goliath down and made him an in-law to King Saul.

3) *"A gift is as a precious stone in the eyes of him that hath it: whithersoever it turneth, it prospereth." (Proverbs 17:8)* We need to appreciate what God has given us to excel in life. Your gift must be precious and valuable to you, if not it will be difficult for you to prosper with it.

Is it possible to neglect the gifts in our life?

> *"Neglect not the gift that is in thee, which was given thee by prophecy, with the laying on of the hands of the presbytery." (1 Timothy 4:14)*

Whenever we neglect anything, it will stop producing or it becomes of no relevance to the owner. It was quite ironic that Paul was exhorting Timothy not to neglect his gift because it might cause him to lose out on God. Ponder the following verses that concluded Paul's advice to Timothy:

> *"Meditate upon these things; give thyself wholly to them; that thy profiting may appear to all. Take heed unto thyself, and unto the doctrine; continue in them: for in doing this thou shalt both save thyself, and them that hear thee." (1 Timothy 4:15, 16)*

Food for thought:

> *"But covet earnestly the best gifts: and yet shew I unto you a more excellent way." (1 Corinthians 12:31)*

When you covet something, it means that you put your desire for that thing into the next gear. For us to have an overflowing and extraordinary life, God has given us the GIFTS advantage. What are your gifts? Your discovery of these gifts will be a good testimony of your love for this God that has given us an advantage in a world that wants us to remain anxious about our lives.

How can we develop and maximize our gifs?
This is what Paul encouraged Timothy to do—to stir up his gift. Do you need to stir up your own gift as well? For the gifts in your life to be of help to you, they must be operational and functional.

These are few tips on how you can stir up your gifts so that you can fully enjoy an overflowing life:

> *"Wherefore I put thee in remembrance that thou stir up the gift of God, which is in thee by the putting on of my hands." (2 Timothy 1:6)*

1. Focus on the strengths God gave you. Concentrating on your strengths will help you fulfill the calling God has put on your life.

2. Exercise your gift. Find something you like to do and that you do well, and do it over and over again. Want to know what will happen? You will feel better about yourself because you won't be constantly failing.

3. Have the courage to be different. Unhappiness comes when you try to be like everyone else rather than embracing the unique person that you are.

4. Learn to cope with criticism. Have enough confidence in who you are in Christ. Listen to others and be open to change without feeling you have to agree with everyone's viewpoint or obtain their approval. (A devotional from Joyce Meyers)

Beware of false gift.

"Whoso boasteth himself of a false gift is like clouds and wind without rain." (Proverbs 25:14)

The recipient of a good gift should not even boast at all let alone the recipient of a false gift—clouds without water. A false gift brings a great loss. Let us consider an example:

"Then certain of the vagabond Jews, exorcists, took upon them to call over them which had evil spirits the name of the Lord Jesus, saying, we adjure you by Jesus whom Paul preacheth. And there were seven sons of one Sceva, a Jew, and chief of the priests, which did so. And the evil spirit answered and said, Jesus I know, and Paul I know; but who are ye? And the man in whom the evil spirit was leaped on them, and overcame them, and prevailed against them, so that they fled out of that house naked and wounded." (Acts 19:13-16)

If you want to operate in Paul's gift then you need to have the discipline and commitment that qualified Paul to function in that gift.

Can spiritual gifts be imparted upon us?

One of the benefits of a spiritual father or mother is their ability to impart into your life whatever gifts you need to excel.

"For I long to see you, that I may impart unto you some spiritual gift, to the end ye may be established;" (Romans 1:11)

"Wherefore I put thee in remembrance that thou stir up the gift of God, which is in thee by the putting on of my hands." (2 Timothy 1:6)

There are several examples in the Bible of such spiritual transactions: Elijah to Elisha, Paul to Timothy and many more. Stay close to your spiritual parents; the rewards are robust!

Are these gifts mine to keep forever?

God's gift to you are irrevocable. Don't let the devil deceive you that when you messed up, God is done with you. If and when we go the wrong path, all we need to do is to repent of that sin, confess, ask for forgiveness and stay close to God without moving farther away.

> *"For God's gifts and His call are irrevocable. He never withdraws them when once they are given, and He does not change His mind about those to whom He gives His grace or to whom He sends His call." (Romans 11:29 AMP)*

Food for thought:

> *"As every man hath received the gift, even so minister the same one to another, as good stewards of the manifold grace of God." (1 Peter 4:10)*

Keep in mind that gifts (like the talents in the Parable of talents) are not distributed by the master equally. To some, He gave one and another two… Stay in your lane and be productive!

CHAPTER 3

THE WORD: RHEMA OR LOGOS?

"Whom shall he teach knowledge? And whom shall he make to understand doctrine? Them that are weaned from the milk, and drawn from the breasts. For precept must be upon precept, precept upon precept; line upon line, line upon line; here a little, and there a little:" (Isaiah 28:9, 10)

I begin this chapter with those questions in the verse above which, I believe, The Lord is asking us today.

To live an extraordinary life is to be skillful in the use of the Word of God. God Himself made a mystifying statement about the knowledge of the word. He said *"My people are destroyed for lack of knowledge: because thou hast rejected knowledge, I will also reject thee, that thou shalt be no priest to me: seeing thou hast forgotten the law of thy God, I will also forget thy children." (Hosea 4:6)*

If an individual is destroyed because of lack of knowledge, then the work of redemption becomes elusive to him or her. To reject knowledge is another level of rebellion, because it is an act of disobedience such as what Eve did in the garden. When we reject knowledge, we ignorantly throw away our priesthood in the act.

Rejection of the word is like beholding our face in a glass and immediately forgetting what we look like.

> *"But be ye doers of the word, and not hearers only, deceiving your own selves. For if any be a hearer of the word, and not a doer, he is like unto a man beholding his natural face in a glass: For he beholdeth himself, and goeth his way, and straightway forgetteth what manner of man he was. But whoso looketh into the perfect law of liberty, and continueth therein, he being not a forgetful hearer, but a doer of the work, this man shall be blessed in his deed." (James 1:22-25)*

The terrifying part of this problem is that it does not only affect you but the coming generations as well. The strong verdict is what the Lord said: I WILL FORGET THY CHILDREN. That is not a joke. We cannot afford to endanger the generation to come because of our ignorance of God's Word. The good news is that God does not want us to think that we have to lock ourselves up somewhere for days in the bid of trying to gain access to His word. His instructions about how to approach the word is this:

> *"For precept must be upon precept, precept, upon precept; line upon line, line upon line; here a little, and there a little:" (Isaiah 28:10)*

Do you get it? It takes constant and persistent effort to gain knowledge; it is here a little and there a little. What are you seeking to get in the word that will give you an extraordinary life? Here is one of many answers:

> *"My son, forget not my law; but let thine heart keep my commandments: For length of days, and long life, and peace, shall they add to thee." (Proverbs 3:1-2)*

God gives instructions to sons and daughters and not strangers. Why ? Because they do not hear His voice.

> *"But Jesus said unto her, Let the children first be filled: for it is not meet to take the children's bread, and to cast it unto the dogs. And she answered and said unto him, Yes, Lord: yet the dogs under the table eat of the children's crumbs." (Mark 7:27-28)*

> *"My sheep hear my voice, and I know them, and they follow me:" (John 10:27)*

So the primary question is: Are you a son or daughter of God? And guess what? You are the only one who can answer that question. If you have not been hearing the voice of Jesus, maybe He does not know you; and if so, how can he influence your life?

When we talk about an extraordinary life, many of us instantly think about money, but Proverbs 3:1-2 highlights three indices of an extraordinary life which many will give up their money to possess:

- Length of Days
- Long life
- Peace

It is the knowledge of the word that will add these to your life.

> *"This book of the law shall not depart out of thy mouth; but thou shalt meditate therein day and night, that thou mayest observe to do according to all that is written therein: for then thou shalt make thy way prosperous, and then thou shalt have good success." (Joshua 1:8)*

If you do according to all that is written, the rewards are inexhaustible!

- Thou shall make thy way prosperous. Notice that it said 'way' and not 'ways'. That's because if you get it right here, all other ways will comply with the word of the Lord.
- Thou shalt have good success. Self-explanatory, isn't it.

...to mention just a few.

> *"Blessed is the man that walketh not in the counsel of the ungodly, nor standeth in the way of sinners, nor sitteth in the seat of the scornful. But his delight is in the law of the Lord; and in his law doth he meditate day and night. And he shall be like a tree planted by the rivers of water, that bringeth forth his fruit in his season; his leaf also shall not wither; and whatsoever he doeth shall prosper. The ungodly are not so: but are like the chaff which the wind driveth away. Therefore the ungodly shall not stand in the judgment, nor sinners in the congregation of the righteous. For the Lord knoweth the way of the righteous: but the way of the ungodly shall perish." (Psalms 1:1-6)*

Food for thought:

> *"Study to shew thyself approved unto God, a workman that needeth not to be ashamed, rightly dividing the*

> *word of truth." (2 Timothy 2:15).*

WE HOLD THESE TRUTH TO BE SELF-EVIDENT

Take a look at this Bible verse:

> *"My son, attend to my words; incline thine ear unto my sayings. Let them not depart from thine eyes; keep them in the midst of thine heart. For they are life unto those that find them, and health to all their flesh." (Proverbs 4:20-22)*

In the constitution of the United States of America, there are three basic unalienable rights endowed us by our Creator (from the study of the word); we hold these truths as an evidence that these rights are granted by God and not men or other evolutionary theories.

"We hold these truths to be self-evident, that all men are created equal, that they are endowed by their Creator with certain unalienable Rights, that among these are Life, Liberty and the pursuit of Happiness"

We'll consider these three one after the other.

1. LIFE

God gives life which is required for man here on earth to enjoy all His creation and a second life which is needed by man to reign with Him in eternity.

The First life

"And the Lord God formed man of the dust of the ground,

and breathed into his nostrils the breath of life; and man became a living soul." (Genesis 2:7)

The Second life

"Jesus answered and said unto him, Verily, verily, I say unto thee, Except a man be born again, he cannot see the kingdom of God. Marvel not that I said unto thee, Ye must be born again." (John 3:3, 7)

"For God so loved the world, that he gave his only begotten Son, that whosoever believeth in him should not perish, but have everlasting life." (John 3:16)

"In him was life; and the life was the light of men. And the light shineth in darkness; and the darkness comprehended it not." (John 1:4, 5)

Both lives come from God. The knowledge of His word places us on the path that grants us a full access to the extraordinary life. The word of God enriches our lives and helps to live right

2. LIBERTY

God gives us liberty. True liberation from oppression comes from His throne. To the people of the world, the term liberty has a lot of different meanings—liberty to sleep with whatsoever or whosoever (which can lead to death), liberty to drink oneself to death, to mention a few. True liberty comes from the Lord.

"And I will walk at liberty: for I seek thy precepts." (Psalms 119:45)

"Now the Lord is that Spirit: and where the Spirit of

the Lord is, there is liberty." (2 Corinthians 3:17)

"But whoso looketh into the perfect law of liberty, and continueth therein, he being not a forgetful hearer, but a doer of the work, this man shall be blessed in his deed." (James 1:25)

3. PURSUIT OF HAPPINESS

God is the only one that can truly make you happy. The richest man who ever lived was Solomon. I believe we can learn few things from his life about the pursuit of happiness. God gave Solomon wisdom—the medium by which we can achieve and live our dream.

"And God gave Solomon wisdom and understanding exceeding much, and largeness of heart, even as the sand that is on the seashore. And Solomon's wisdom excelled the wisdom of all the children of the east country, and all the wisdom of Egypt. For he was wiser than all men; than Ethan the Ezrahite, and Heman, and Chalcol, and Darda, the sons of Mahol: and his fame was in all nations round about." (1 Kings 4:29-31)

Wisdom is pivotal.

"Wisdom is the principal thing; therefore get wisdom: and with all thy getting get understanding. Exalt her, and she shall promote thee: she shall bring thee to honour, when thou dost embrace her. She shall give to thine head an ornament of grace: a crown of glory shall she deliver to thee." (Proverbs 4:7-9)

"Through skillful and godly Wisdom is a house" (a life, a home, a family) built, and by understanding it is established [on a sound and good foundation], And by

> *knowledge shall its chambers [of every area] be filled with all precious and pleasant riches." (Proverbs 24:3-4 AMP)*

All these will result into an extraordinary life, and they all come from being grounded in the word of God.

*Food for though*t:

> *"Thy word is a lamp unto my feet, and a light unto my path." (Psalms 119:105)*

If you have a good lamp, your path will continue to shine brighter and brighter and you will have good success. You begin to locate God's covenant promises to you from His word and put Him to remembrance of them.

> *"My covenant will I not break, nor alter the thing that is gone out of my lips." (Psalms 89:34)*

To fully enjoy and have an extraordinary life, it is highly imperative that we know what is written about us. For a will to be executed, the contents of that will have to be made known to the benefactors. It is impossible for a benefactor to say that he has gotten all that belongs to him if what was written in the will has not been made known.

What is written about you?

> *"Then said I, Lo, I come: in the volume of the book it is written of me, I delight to do thy will, O my God: yea, thy law is within my heart." (Psalms 40:7, 8)*

What has been written about you is not a page; what God has in stock is in volume of books and you need to dig in and find out all the promises tagged after your name so that you can activate your many blessings. That is a great way to enjoy your extraordinary life.

Abraham knew what God said about him and he stood his ground until every bit of the promises were fulfilled.

> *"He staggered not at the promise of God through unbelief; but was strong in faith, giving glory to God; And being fully persuaded that, what he had promised, he was able also to perform. And therefore it was imputed to him for righteousness." (Romans 4:20-22)*

The truth that you know is the truth that will set you free. You need to look into the book to find some truth about your future and destiny.

> *"And ye shall know the truth, and the truth shall make you free." (John 8:32)*

Here are few tips to improve your study time with God (adopted from Joyce Meyers daily devotional):

1. Purposely set aside time. I make an appointment with God in the mornings, but if that doesn't work for you, find a time that does, even if it's not every day. Just start somewhere and you'll see the positive fruit that this time brings to your life!

2. Make preparation for your Bible study. Choose a place you like and where you can be undisturbed (e.g. a room in your house where you can be alone).

3. Have all your materials available. You'll want your Bible, of course, but also get a good Bible dictionary, concordance, pen and paper. That way, it's easier to reference something or write something down.

4. Prepare your heart. Talk to God about things you may need to confess, and enter your study time peacefully and without anything that may block you from receiving revelation during your study.

Food for thought:

> *"Blessed are they that do his commandments, that they may have right to the tree of life, and may enter in through the gates into the city." (Revelation 22:14)*

When you know his commandments from the study of the word, you have the right to the tree of life.

CHAPTER 4

ABOUNDING IN WISDOM

"Wisdom is the principal thing; therefore get wisdom: and with all thy getting get understanding." (Proverbs 4:7)

ABOUNDING IN WISDOM

The supremacy of wisdom in living a running-over life cannot be overemphasized.

"Happy is the man that findeth wisdom, and the man that getteth understanding. For the merchandise of it is better than the merchandise of silver, and the gain thereof than fine gold. She is more precious than rubies: and all the things thou canst desire are not to be compared unto her. Length of days is in her right hand; and in her left hand riches and honour. Her ways are ways of pleasantness, and all her paths are peace. She is a tree of life to them that lay hold upon her: and happy is every one that retaineth her. The Lord by wisdom hath

> *founded the earth; by understanding hath he established the heavens. By his knowledge the depths are broken up, and the clouds drop down the dew. My son, let not them depart from thine eyes: keep sound wisdom and discretion:" (Proverbs 3:13-21)*

Wisdom helps us to build our lives because of all it adds to us. Just like any house built; there are needs for pillars so that when the storms of life blow, these pillars will remain standing and with that we continue to enjoy our extraordinary life.

> *"Wisdom hath builded her house, she hath hewn out her seven pillars:" (Proverbs 9:1)*

What are these seven essential pillars that we must build our lives on through Wisdom?

1. Prudence
2. Knowledge
3. Discretion
4. Counsel
5. Sound Judgement
6. Understanding
7. Power

Let us examine at these seven essential pillars one after the other:

1. PRUDENCE

It means doing the right thing. This is the first pillar that wisdom builds on. Anywhere you see wisdom, you see right doing and right living. The right thing to do is for us to have a heart to build the kingdom of God, because when we seek the kingdom first, every other thing shall be added unto us.

"Huram said moreover, blessed be the Lord God of Israel, that made heaven and earth, who hath given to David the king a wise son, endued with prudence and understanding that might build a house for the Lord, and a house for his kingdom." (2 Chronicles 2:12)

> *"I wisdom dwell with prudence, and find out knowledge of witty inventions." (Proverbs 8:12)*

2. KNOWLEDGE

It means finding the truth for wisdom to make our lives better. The Bible says my people perish for lack of knowledge. Wisdom will always lead us to the truth, that is why Solomon encouraged us repeatedly in his book of Proverbs to keep the word as the focus of our lives.

> *"The proverbs of Solomon the son of David, king of Israel; To know wisdom and instruction; to perceive the words of understanding; To receive the instruction of wisdom, justice, and judgment, and equity; To give subtilty to the simple, to the young man knowledge and discretion. A wise man will hear, and will increase learning; and a man of understanding shall attain unto wise counsels:" (Proverbs 1:1-5)*

Food for thought:

"Wisdom comes in instalments and is available to all who are ready to ask, study God's Word and walk closer with the Spirit of God – who is the Spirit of Wisdom. How do you get wisdom? First it is by getting information." (Pastor E A Adeboye)

3. DISCRETION

It is consideration and acting based on conviction and according to the truth. Discretion is a gift from God and the ability to use it to choose right comes from the guidance of the Holy Spirit.

"For his God doth instruct him to discretion, and doth teach him." (Isaiah 28:26)

"When wisdom entereth into thine heart, and knowledge is pleasant unto thy soul; Discretion shall preserve thee, understanding shall keep thee:" (Proverbs 2:10-11)

"Discretion shall preserve thee"; what a thought! With the right use of your discretion your life will be preserved. Can you remember any incidence when you failed to exercise the use of discretion? What was the cost?

"My son, let not them depart from thine eyes: keep sound wisdom and discretion: So shall they be life unto thy soul, and grace to thy neck. Then shalt thou walk in thy way safely, and thy foot shall not stumble. When thou liest down, thou shalt not be afraid: yea, thou shalt lie down, and thy sleep shall be sweet." (Proverbs 3:21-24)

Discretion will make grace a necklace to you, you will walk safely, you will be stable and you will have sweet sleep.

"The discretion of a man deferreth his anger; and it is his glory to pass over a transgression." (Proverbs 19:11)

Discretion will keep you from transgression when it helps you deal with your anger. Discretion is the only thing that can make it possible for you to be angry and sin not.

"My son, attend unto my wisdom, and bow thine ear to my understanding: That thou mayest regard discretion, and that thy lips may keep knowledge." (Proverbs 5:1-2)

When you use discretion well you will be able to retain knowledge.

"A good man sheweth favour, and lendeth: he will guide his affairs with discretion." (Psalms 112:5)

Guide your affairs with discretion; it is like having the gift of discernment, so use it on all occasion.

4. COUNSEL

This is having a sense of purpose with unity. You experience the peace that passes all understanding when you receive wise counsel.

And where does counsel comes from?

"Counsel is mine, and sound wisdom: I am understanding; I have strength." (Proverbs 8:14)

"With him is wisdom and strength, he hath counsel and understanding." (Job 12:13)

"The counsel of the Lord standeth forever, the thoughts of his heart to all generations." (Psalms 33:11)

Sound counsel comes only from the Lord and His word. Any counsel from any other source should be judged based on the word of God.

Food for thought:

> *"If any of you lack wisdom, let him ask of God, that giveth to all men liberally, and upbraided not; and it shall be given him. But let him ask in faith, nothing wavering. For he that wavereth is like a wave of the sea driven with the wind and tossed." (James 1:5, 6)*

The key word here is that God gives to ALL men (and women) liberally! If you are human, then you qualify for wisdom and all the seven pillars.

> *"Let me give you some good advice; I'm looking you in the eye and giving it to you straight:" (Psalm 32:8 MSG)*

The good news is that God is able and willing to give us some pieces of good advice.

> *"Where no counsel is, the people fall: but in the multitude of counsellors there is safety." (Proverbs 11:14)*

"The people fall." A fall can be devastating. One may not even recover from it. If you look back and count the number of times you have fallen, you should answer for yourself whether you sought counsel of the Lord or not.

There are three main areas where we must seek the counsel of the Lord.

- **Marriage**

Let us take for an example the case of Isaac:

> *"And Abraham was old, and well stricken in age: and the Lord had blessed Abraham in all things. And Abraham said unto his eldest servant of his house, that ruled over all that he had, Put, I pray thee, thy hand*

under my thigh: And I will make thee swear by the Lord, the God of heaven, and the God of the earth, that thou shalt not take a wife unto my son of the daughters of the Canaanites, among whom I dwell: But thou shalt go unto my country, and to my kindred, and take a wife unto my son Isaac." (Genesis 24:1-4)

If a man or woman chooses the wrong partner in marriage, the consequence can be devastating. If you start incorrectly, it will end erroneously. (More on this in my book titled "I AM THREE DIMENSIONAL", it will provide you with biblical insights on how to choose the God's way).

"Be ye not unequally yoked together with unbelievers: for what fellowship hath righteousness with unrighteousness? And what communion hath light with darkness? And what concord hath Christ with Belial? Or what part hath he that believeth with an infidel? And what agreement hath the temple of God with idols? For ye are the temple of the living God; as God hath said, I will dwell in them, and walk in them; and I will be their God, and they shall be my people." (2 Corinthians 6:14-16)

- **Career**

There might not be a specific scripture that tells you the particular career you should choose, but let us look at this good example of how you can know what you are cut out for. (My book titled "I AM THREE DIMENSIONAL" can provide some help in this area as well).

"For the kingdom of heaven is as a man travelling into a far country, who called his own servants, and delivered unto them his goods. And unto one he gave five talents,

to another two, and to another one; to every man according to his several ability; and straightway took his journey." (Matthew 25:14-15)

You need to identify which group you fall into. A one-talent guy can't find fulfillment pulling a two-talent guy's responsibilities nor a five-talent guy find fulfilment producing at a two-talents level. You need to come to terms with your capacity.

- **Where you choose to live**

This is equally of utmost importance because if you get it right in the first two areas and you miss it here, it can be very disastrous. Let us look at the scriptures:

"The earth is the Lord's, and the fullness thereof; the world, and they that dwell therein." (Psalms 24:1).

Since the earth belongs to God, then He can tell you where you will thrive. When you have a guest come over to see you as the host, you will determine what room your guest is going to sleep in. The reason for your choice of the room to sleep might be because you know certain things about your guest. Likewise, we are God's guests on this planet; let Him tell us where we should stay. Do not relocate just because you think there are better opportunities where you are relocating to. That was an error Isaac made.

"And there was a famine in the land, beside the first famine that was in the days of Abraham. And Isaac went unto Abimelech king of the Philistines unto Gerar. And the Lord appeared unto him, and said, Go not down into Egypt; dwell in the land which I shall tell thee of: And Isaac dwelt in Gerar: Then Isaac sowed in that land, and received in the same year an hundredfold:

and the Lord blessed him. And the man waxed great, and went forward, and grew until he became very great:" (Genesis 26:1, 2, 6, 12, 13)

"Without counsel purposes are disappointed: but in the multitude of counsellors they are established." (Proverbs 15:22)

You should be able to answer the questions of:

- what am I here for?
- what is my purpose?

Here is your answer! You can find your purpose by following his complete counsel and your determination will not be disappointed.

Food for thought:

"Blessed is the man that walketh not in the counsel of the ungodly, nor standeth in the way of sinners, nor sitteth in the seat of the scornful." (Psalms 1:1)

The sure way to attract God's blessing is to walk in His counsel.

There are some other areas where we must seek the guidance and counsel of the Lord. The stories below illustrate this.

"And they said unto him, From a very far country thy servants are come because of the name of the Lord thy God: for we have heard the fame of him, and all that he did in Egypt, And all that he did to the two kings of the Amorites, that were beyond Jordan, to Sihon king of Heshbon, and to Og king of Bashan, which was at

> *Ashtaroth. Wherefore our elders and all the inhabitants of our country spake to us, saying, Take victuals with you for the journey, and go to meet them, and say unto them, We are your servants: therefore now make ye a league with us. This our bread we took hot for our provision out of our houses on the day we came forth to go unto you; but now, behold, it is dry, and it is mouldy: And these bottles of wine, which we filled, were new; and, behold, they be rent: and these our garments and our shoes are become old by reason of the very long journey. And the men took of their victuals, and asked not counsel at the mouth of the Lord. And Joshua made peace with them, and made a league with them, to let them live: and the princes of the congregation sware unto them." (Joshua 9:9-15)*

In this story, the Israelites formed an association with strange people. Joshua had established an association which turned out to be a very wrong one. He simply did not seek God's counsel before he accepted their friendship. How many associations have you formed that has resulted in disaster? Look before you leap, for not all that glitters is gold!

Here is another story:

> *"And Saul said, Let us go down after the Philistines by night, and spoil them until the morning light, and let us not leave a man of them. And they said, Do whatsoever seemeth good unto thee. Then said the priest, Let us draw near hither unto God. And Saul asked counsel of God, Shall I go down after the Philistines? wilt thou deliver them into the hand of Israel? But he answered him not that day." (1 Samuel 14:36-37)*

Here Saul asked for God's counsel—he did well but the Bible says "But he answered him not that day". There will be times when we ask for God's counsel and he will not answer immediately. What are we supposed to do? We keep waiting until He tells us to move. That is, there is an element of time. Here is what Jesus told the Apostles before He left and following this counsel really put all their ministries in high gear:

> *"And, being assembled together with them, commanded them that they should not depart from Jerusalem, but WAIT for the promise of the Father, which, saith he, ye have heard of me." (Acts 1:4)*

Who can give us counsel?

I believe sincerely that every man or woman must have three fathers—a spiritual father, an earthly father and a father-in-law. If you are fortunate that all these fathers are in the Lord, you can receive Godly counsel from them, and if not you can find a replacement for any of them. When you get counsel from anybody, weigh it on these three things:

1. Is it in line with the word of God?
2. Is there any fruit in the life of my counselor?
3. Does it bear witness to what you think the Lord has told you?

You must remember that "in the mouth of two or three witnesses let every truth be established." It all begins with you being sincere with yourself.

Food for thought:

> *"They soon forgat his works; they waited not for his counsel:" (Psalms 106:13)*

The main reason why people do not wait for God's counsel is because they quickly forget what the Lord has done for them in the past. Please remember all the Lord has done and is still doing and request for His counsel in small and big matters. May the Lord bless you and make His face to shine upon you. AMEN!

5. SOUND JUDGEMENT

This is simply the ability to make right decision—the ability to determine right from wrong. Moses exercised this.

> *"And Moses sent them to spy out the land of Canaan, and said unto them, Get you up this way southward, and go up into the mountain: And see the land, what it is; and the people that dwelleth therein, whether they be strong or weak, few or many; And what the land is that they dwell in, whether it be good or bad; and what cities they be that they dwell in, whether in tents, or in strongholds; And what the land is, whether it be fat or lean, whether there be wood therein, or not. And be ye of good courage, and bring of the fruit of the land. Now the time was the time of the firstripe grapes." (Numbers 13:17-20)*

Moses gave a very specific instruction about what the Lord had told him. True, God has given them the land, but Moses went through what we call due diligence in the business world. Moses demonstrated sound judgement. Anytime you follow the word completely, you are definitely working in sound judgement.

As for the 12 spies, however; they did exactly what Moses

asked of them but they decided to use their judgement to see what the Lord has already called theirs. Whenever your judgement about a situation goes contrary to the word of God, there will always be problem.

> *"So they went up, and searched the land from the wilderness of Zin unto Rehob, as men come to Hamath. And they returned from searching of the land after forty days. And they told him, and said, We came unto the land whither thou sentest us, and surely it floweth with milk and honey; and this is the fruit of it. Nevertheless the people be strong that dwell in the land, and the cities are walled, and very great: and moreover we saw the children of Anak there." (Numbers 13:21, 25, 27, 28)*

10 out of 12 used their sight-based judgements; they completely forgot that "we walk by faith, not by sight" (2 Corinthians 5:7). If you are the type that always follows the majority in any decision making, beware you might be missing out. In this case, the minority (Joshua and Caleb) were the only ones with sound judgement.

> *"And Caleb stilled the people before Moses, and said, Let us go up at once, and possess it; for we are well able to overcome it." (Numbers 13:30)*

What killed the sound judgement of the 10? Their eyesight!

> *"And there we saw the giants, the sons of Anak, which come of the giants: and we were in our own sight as grasshoppers, and so we were in their sight." (Numbers 13:33)*

To live an extraordinary life, your eyesight must be secondary to your inner eyes.

Food for thought:

> *"And Jesus answered him, saying, It is written, That man shall not live by bread alone, but by every word of God." (Luke 4:4)*

If you follow every word of God and not being selective to what interests you only, but rather use sound judgement, you will go far with God.

Let us look into an interesting comparison of the first Adam and the last Adam about the counsel of God given to them. We do not need to look too far to find God's judgement, because they are everywhere. All we need to do is to carry out His counsel using sound judgement. If He is your Lord, then it will be easy to see His counsel, because it will be written on your heart. But if He is not your God yet, then you need to accept Him as your Lord and Savior and pray unto Him to reveal Himself to you.

> *"He is the Lord our God: his judgments are in all the earth." (Psalms 105:7)*

The First Adam:

The counsel of God to the first Adam is this:

> *"And the Lord God took the man, and put him into the garden of Eden to dress it and to keep it. And the Lord God commanded the man, saying, Of every tree of the garden thou mayest freely eat: But of the tree of the knowledge of good and evil, thou shalt not eat of it: for in the day that thou eatest thereof thou shalt surely die." (Genesis 2:15-17)*

The sound judgement here is to keep to what God has said in mind and obey it. When we engage in a conversation with the serpent with our guard down we are heading for a big problem. For you to use your judgement instead of sound judgement, the serpent will always twist the word, it is up to you to be discerning.

> *"Keep thy heart with all diligence; for out of it are the issues of life." (Proverbs 4:23)*

> *"Now the serpent was more subtle than any beast of the field which the Lord God had made. And he said unto the woman, Yea, hath God said, Ye shall not eat of every tree of the garden? And the woman said unto the serpent, We may eat of the fruit of the trees of the garden: But of the fruit of the tree which is in the midst of the garden, God hath said, Ye shall not eat of it, neither shall ye touch it, lest ye die. For God doth know that in the day ye eat thereof, then your eyes shall be opened, and ye shall be as gods, knowing good and evil. And when the woman saw that the tree was good for food, and that it was pleasant to the eyes, and a tree to be desired to make one wise, she took of the fruit thereof, and did eat, and gave also unto her husband with her; and he did eat." (Genesis 3:1-3, 5-6)*

Eve overruled sound judgement by her canal judgement.

> *"And when the woman SAW that the tree was good for food, and that it was pleasant to the eyes, and a tree to be desired to make one wise, she took of the fruit thereof, and did eat, and gave also unto her husband with her; and he did eat. (Genesis 3: 6)*

Do not walk by sight; it is very dangerous. Your canal vision will always (not sometimes) change the counsel of God. From this lack of sound judgement, human race became doomed; but thank God for the last Adam. We shall consider how Jesus (our senior brother) handled the same situation with sound judgement.

Food for thought:

> *"Seven times a day do I praise thee because of thy righteous judgments." (Psalms 119:164)*

Let us praise God always for his kindness to us all, allowing us to use sound judgements through obedience to his counsel.

The Last Adam:

The Last Adam is Jesus Christ, our precious Savior. God breathed into the First Adam the breath of life, and He gave him the same spirit like that of Jesus which should have helped him, but he was careless and was not watchful. Adam's temptation took place in a controlled environment (in the garden of Eden). Jesus' temptation took place in the wilderness where anything could have happened.

> *"And the Lord God formed man of the dust of the ground, and breathed into his nostrils the breath of life; and man became a living soul." (Genesis 2:7)*

> *"And Jesus being full of the Holy Ghost returned from Jordan, and was led by the Spirit into the wilderness, Being forty days tempted of the devil. And in those days he did eat nothing: and when they were ended, he afterward hungered. And the devil said unto him, If thou be the Son of God, command this stone that it be made bread. And Jesus answered him, saying, It is written, That man shall not live by bread alone, but by every word of God. And the devil, taking him up into*

an high mountain, shewed unto him all the kingdoms of the world in a moment of time. And the devil said unto him, All this power will I give thee, and the glory of them: for that is delivered unto me; and to whomsoever I will I give it. If thou therefore wilt worship me, all shall be thine. And Jesus answered and said unto him, Get thee behind me, Satan: for it is written, Thou shalt worship the Lord thy God, and him only shalt thou serve. And he brought him to Jerusalem, and set him on a pinnacle of the temple, and said unto him, If thou be the Son of God, cast thyself down from hence: For it is written, He shall give his angels charge over thee, to keep thee: And in their hands they shall bear thee up, lest at any time thou dash thy foot against a stone. And Jesus answering said unto him, It is said, Thou shalt not tempt the Lord thy God. And when the devil had ended all the temptation, he departed from him for a season." (Luke 4:1-13)

The more I carefully study this, the more I discover the need for us to allow ourselves to be filled with the Holy Ghost. Jesus did not eat anything for 40 days and He used the written word to fend off the use of canal judgement.

We can draw out three inferences that helped Jesus to apply sound judgement:

- Be full of the Holy Ghost.
- Live a fasted life.
- Use the written word.

When you succeed at using your sound judgement, you will become famous in the kingdom of darkness and in the world at large.

> *"And Jesus returned in the power of the Spirit into Galilee: and there went out a fame of him through all the region round about." (Luke 4:14)*

Food for thought:

> *"He that hath an ear, let him hear what the Spirit saith unto the churches; To him that overcometh will I give to eat of the tree of life, which is in the midst of the paradise of God. He that hath an ear, let him hear what the Spirit saith unto the churches; He that overcometh shall not be hurt of the second death." (Revelation 2:7, 11)*

This is the use of inner ear to hear and use sound judgement to execute God's counsel. We will eat of the tree of life in the midst of paradise (heaven on earth) and most importantly we shall not be touched by the second death. I want some of that!

It brings to mind the story of Naaman who had leprosy and had tried the best medicine in the world at that time. He was a very wealthy man of war, but could not live an extraordinary life. So what did he do?

> *"And the king of Syria said, Go to, go, and I will send a letter unto the king of Israel. And he departed, and took with him ten talents of silver, and six thousand pieces of gold, and ten changes of raiment. And he brought the letter to the king of Israel, saying, Now when this letter is come unto thee, behold, I have therewith sent Naaman my servant to thee, that thou mayest recover him of his leprosy. And it came to pass, when the king of Israel had read the letter, that he rent his clothes, and said, Am I God, to kill and to make alive,*

that this man doth send unto me to recover a man of his leprosy? wherefore consider, I pray you, and see how he seeketh a quarrel against me. And it was so, when Elisha the man of God had heard that the king of Israel had rent his clothes, that he sent to the king, saying, Wherefore hast thou rent thy clothes? let him come now to me, and he shall know that there is a prophet in Israel. So Naaman came with his horses and with his chariot, and stood at the door of the house of Elisha. And Elisha sent a messenger unto him, saying, Go and wash in Jordan seven times, and thy flesh shall come again to thee, and thou shalt be clean. But Naaman was wroth, and went away, and said, Behold, I thought, He will surely come out to me, and stand, and call on the name of the Lord his God, and strike his hand over the place, and recover the leper. Are not Abana and Pharpar, rivers of Damascus, better than all the waters of Israel? may I not wash in them, and be clean? So he turned and went away in a rage. And his servants came near, and spake unto him, and said, My father, if the prophet had bid thee do some great thing, wouldest thou not have done it? how much rather then, when he saith to thee, Wash, and be clean? Then went he down, and dipped himself seven times in Jordan, according to the saying of the man of God: and his flesh came again like unto the flesh of a little child, and he was clean." (2 Kings 5:5-14)

Lessons from the story:

- When the letter came from the king of Syria to the king of Israel, the conventional wisdom or the canal judgement is for the king to step into the role of a prophet. After all, Saul the king stepped into the role of a prophet—and missed it. This king demonstrated the use of sound judgement in recognizing his calling as a king and not as a prophet. The lesson for us all is to always recognize our calling, since KINGS and PRIESTS have different callings and functions altogether.

- Naaman thought the man of God will come to the door and laid his hands upon him. How many times has our thought limited us to our canal judgement instead of using sound judgement? The ten spies and Eve saw things that changed their destiny forever. Likewise, Naaman's thought was about to destroy him for life; thank God for the servant that persuaded him to use sound judgement in following the prophet's instructions. Two things to watch out for are our sights and our thoughts. Both of these can easily take us down a path that can limit our potentials.

- God's commandments may not occasionally make sense to our canal judgement, but all you need to do is to just obey.

- Naaman was cleansed from his leprosy. When we use sound judgement, it will always result into cleanliness all around in our finances, spiritual and family lives.

On the other hand let us look at Gehazi's life.

"But he said, As the Lord liveth, before whom I stand, I will receive none. And he urged him to take it; but he refused. And he said unto him, Go in peace. So he departed from him a little way. But Gehazi, the servant of Elisha the man of God, said, Behold, my master hath spared Naaman this Syrian, in not receiving at his hands

> *that which he brought: but, as the Lord liveth, I will run after him, and take somewhat of him. But he went in, and stood before his master. And Elisha said unto him, whence comest thou, Gehazi? And he said, Thy servant went no whither. The leprosy therefore of Naaman shall cleave unto thee, and unto thy seed forever. And he went out from his presence a leper as white as snow." (2 Kings 5:16, 19, 20, 25, 27)*

The sound judgement here was for Gehazi to abide by what the prophet had declared as God's counsel but he exercised his own judgement. The result of that decision was devastating.

> *"The leprosy of Naaman shall cleave unto you and your seed forever, because of the use of canal judgement,he brought leprosy to the yet unborn generation." (2 Kings 5: 27)*

Food for thought:

Every form of leprosy that has come upon you because of lack of sound judgement in your generation, we plead the blood of Jesus and you are released in Jesus Name, AMEN!

6. UNDERSTANDING

Understanding applied knowledge; a superior power of discernment; enlightened intelligence or familiarity with a particular thing. It could also mean skill in dealing with or handling something…and it only comes from God.

> *"Then opened he their understanding, that they might understand the scriptures," (Luke 24:45)*

"But there is a spirit in man: and the inspiration of the Almighty giveth them understanding." (Job 32:8)

"The fear of the Lord is the beginning of wisdom: and the knowledge of the holy is understanding." (Proverbs 9:10)

"The entrance of thy words giveth light; it giveth understanding unto the simple." (Psalms 119:130)

If God can open one's understanding, then it goes without saying that understanding can be closed as well. When we operate with closed understanding, then it becomes very difficult to know our season when it comes upon us. The knowledge of the Holy Spirit is understanding. When we look into the perfect law of liberty, we will have light, and the light in return brings understanding.

What do we need to understand?

"And of the children of Issachar, which were men that had understanding of the times, to know what Israel ought to do; the heads of them were two hundred; and all their brethren were at their commandment." (1 Chronicles 12:32)

"Wherefore be ye not unwise, but understanding what the will of the Lord is." (Ephesians 5:17)

"What is it then? I will pray with the spirit, and I will pray with the understanding also: I will sing with the spirit, and I will sing with the understanding also." (1 Corinthians 14:15)

When you have the understanding of the times, you will know your season, when you know your season, you will definitely know the will of God. When you know the will of God, you will be able to pray accordingly and the result will be an extraordinary life.

Food for thought:

> *"Good understanding giveth favour: but the way of transgressors is hard." (Proverbs 13:15)*

> *"Wisdom is the principal thing; therefore get wisdom: and with all thy getting get understanding." (Proverbs 4:7)*

People, with all thy getting get understanding!

> *"Trust in the Lord with all thine heart; and lean not unto thine own understanding. Happy is the man that findeth wisdom, and the man that getteth understanding." (Proverbs 3:5, 13)*

The key word in that verse is for us not to LEAN on our own understanding. To LEAN is to incline or bend (especially in feeling, opinion, or action), or to rest against or on something for support, to depend or rely.

Daniel's story comes to mind.

> *"Children in whom was no blemish, but well favoured, and skilful in all wisdom, and cunning in knowledge, and understanding science, and such as had ability in them to stand in the king's palace, and whom they might teach the learning and the tongue of the Chaldeans. But Daniel purposed in his heart that he would not defile himself with the portion of the king's meat, nor with the wine which he drank: therefore he requested of the prince of the eunuchs that he might not defile himself. Prove thy servants, I beseech thee, ten days; and let them give us pulse to eat, and water to drink. And in all matters*

> *of wisdom and understanding, that the king enquired of them, he found them ten times better than all the magicians and astrologers that were in all his realm." (Daniel 1:4, 8, 12, 20)*

The normal rule and understanding was for Daniel to eat of the king's portion which was the norm, but he was a man that will bend from that worldly understanding to lean towards eating 'pulse' instead of the king's portion and the result was evident that he operated in divine understanding of heavenly principles. How many believers have defiled themselves in politics, leaning on their own understanding instead of bending towards the vertical position of Godly understanding.

Daniel excelled. He was able to avert the death of all the wise men in the kingdom. The king had a dream but forgot it entirely, he was not only asking them to interpret the dream but to tell him of the dream he had.

> *"And the king said unto them, I have dreamed a dream, and my spirit was troubled to know the dream. For this cause the king was angry and very furious, and commanded to destroy all the wise men of Babylon. He answered and said to Arioch the king's captain, Why is the decree so hasty from the king? Then Arioch made the thing known to Daniel." (Daniel 2:3, 12, 15)*

God did not only reveal the dream to Daniel, but gave him the understanding to interpret the dream. Understanding will bring you into honor and promote you. Let us ask God for uncommon understanding of His mind for our generation. If we understand His mandate, it will be easy to walk with God like Enoch did, whom He took away without tasting death. May we all grow to that depth of Understanding in Jesus name.

> *"And Enoch walked with God: and he was not; for God took him." (Genesis 5:24)*

One of the biblical characters that demonstrated divine understanding is Solomon.

> *"Behold, I have done according to thy words: lo, I have given thee a wise and an understanding heart; so that there was none like thee before thee, neither after thee shall any arise like unto thee." (1 Kings 3:12)*

The story of the two harlots and their dispute over a living and a dead baby is a practical application of knowledge—divine understanding

> *"And the king said, Bring me a sword. And they brought a sword before the king. And the king said, Divide the living child in two, and give half to the one, and half to the other. Then spake the woman whose the living child was unto the king, for her bowels yearned upon her son, and she said, O my lord, give her the living child, and in no wise slay it. But the other said, Let it be neither mine nor thine, but divide it. Then the king answered and said, Give her the living child, and in no wise slay it: she is the mother thereof. And all Israel heard of the judgment which the king had judged; and they feared the king: for they saw that the wisdom of God was in him, to do judgment." (1 Kings 3:24-28)*

Food for thought:

> *"If any of you lack wisdom, let him ask of God, that giveth to all men liberally, and upbraideth not; and it*

> *shall be given him. But let him ask in faith, nothing wavering. For he that wavereth is like a wave of the sea driven with the wind and tossed." (James 1:5, 6)*

Solomon asked God for understanding and he got it. Ask Him today as well.

7. POWER

Power is the ability to act; the capability of doing or accomplishing something. It is a great or marked ability to do or act; strength; might; force. It's also the possession of control or command over others or a legal ability, capacity, or authority: the power of attorney.

The Bible tells us that Jesus is the wisdom and power of God. Wherever we see wisdom, power is always available. Jesus said ALL POWER in heaven and on earth is given unto Him. Why? Because He grew in wisdom and physique. As we grow in size, our measure of wisdom should increase unless we are not true followers of the Master. We pray for favor a lot but it should come natural to us as we increase in wisdom and stature. If it is not in this order then something is missing. Wisdom determines how fast you grow and how much favor is available to you.

That sequence can easily be inferred from the life of Jesus; first, *"...Jesus increased in wisdom and stature, and in favour with God and man." (Luke 2:52) Then "...Jesus came and spake unto them, saying, All power is given unto me in heaven and in earth." (Matthew 28:18)*

Interestingly, the Bible says that "Wisdom strengtheneth the wise more than ten mighty men which are in the city."

(Ecclesiastes 7:19) In order words, wisdom releases power in the exponent of 10. That's amazing! In mathematics, 10 to power of 10 is 100, now it is obvious to see the reason why wisdom builds on power, the power it produces makes you ten times efficient. Daniel and the 3 Hebrews confirmed this for, by virtue of God's wisdom upon their lives, they became ten times better than their equals.

Food for thought:

> *"Labour not to be rich: cease from thine own wisdom." (Proverbs 23:4)*

Riches or wealth does not come by much labor, it is produced by the power that the wisdom of God enables you to generate.

Having shared this much on the seven pillars of wisdom, let's conclude with the dictionary meaning of wisdom.

WISDOM is "The quality or state of being wise; knowledge of what is true or right coupled with just judgment as to action; sagacity, discernment, or insight."

Solomon was the only king that asked God for wisdom, and after studying his life, I can comprehend how he lived such an extraordinary life effortlessly.

> *"In that night did God appear unto Solomon, and said unto him, ask what I shall give thee. And Solomon said unto God, Thou hast shewed great mercy unto David my father, and hast made me to reign in his stead. Now, O Lord God, let thy promise unto David my father be established: for thou hast made me king over a people like the dust of the earth in multitude. Give me now wisdom and knowledge that I may go out and come in*

before this people: for who can judge this thy people that is so great? And God said to Solomon, Because this was in thine heart, and thou hast not asked riches, wealth, or honor, nor the life of thine enemies, neither yet hast asked long life; but hast asked wisdom and knowledge for thyself, that thou mayest judge my people, over whom I have made thee king: Wisdom and knowledge is granted unto thee; and I will give thee riches, and wealth, and honor, such as none of the kings have had that have been before thee, neither shall there any after thee have the like." (2 Chronicles 1:7-12)

Solomon asked God for wisdom and he got a lot more. He got so much wealth and influence because the power to these is released through the application of wisdom—not from physical strength.

"And thou say in thine heart, My power and the might of mine hand hath gotten me this wealth. But thou shalt remember the Lord thy God: for it is he that giveth thee power to get wealth, that he may establish his covenant which he sware unto thy fathers, as it is this day." (Deuteronomy 8:17, 18)

Solomon is the only king that never fought any war though he had a mighty army and he ruled for forty years. Brethren, the power to maintain peace comes from wisdom! It is very easy to avoid conflict by the power of wisdom.

"And king Solomon passed all the kings of the earth in riches and wisdom. And all the kings of the earth sought the presence of Solomon, to hear his wisdom, that God had put in his heart. And they brought every man his present, vessels of silver, and vessels of gold, and raiment,

> *harness, and spices, horses, and mules, a rate year by year. And Solomon had four thousand stalls for horses and chariots, and twelve thousand horsemen; whom he bestowed in the chariot cities, and with the king at Jerusalem." (2 Chronicles 9:22-25)*

Food for thought:

> *"I wisdom dwell with prudence, and find out knowledge of witty inventions." (Proverbs 8:12)*

To be witty is to be amusingly clever in perception and expression—and that comes from the power of wisdom. With all thy getting, get wisdom.

CHAPTER 5

THE POWER OF VISION

WHAT IS VISION?

Different dictionaries said different things about vision. Vision is the act or power of sensing with the eyes—sight. It is the act or power of anticipating that which will or may come to be (eg. prophetic vision; the vision of an entrepreneur). Vision is an experience in which a personage, thing, or event appears vividly or credibly to the mind, although not actually present, often under the influence of a divine intervention; something seen or otherwise perceived during such an experience. Vision usually reveals its message in a vivid form. It can also be an imaginative conception or anticipation and it may be visions of wealth and glory.

One of many definitions of vision is the power of sensing with the eyes; having a good sight. This is very much needed to move our life forward. And vision, as we discuss in this sense for a believer is not the ability of a good natural sight, rather it is the sensing of God's timing, using one's inner eyes and executing life's tasks accordingly. Our understanding from the Bible is that "we do not walk by sight but by faith". Having a good vision for one's life is an act of faith not to be taken with levity. Vision has a voice and it speaks! It is not just a written word, because Paul made it clear that "the letter kills"; it is faith that gives life to your vision. When you have vision, it will develop a passion in you which will set you on a mission to accomplish great and mighty things.

> *"(For we walk by faith, not by sight!" (2 Corinthians 5:7).*

> *"For the letter killeth, but the spirit giveth life." (2 Corinthians 3:6b)*

Food for thought:

A Japanese proverb says that a vision without action is daydream. Action without vision is nightmare.

> *"And the earth was without form, and void; and darkness was upon the face of the deep. And the Spirit of God moved upon the face of the waters." (Genesis 1:2)*

It is evident from creation that God is a God of vision. He created the earth in six days and rested on the seventh. When the earth was without form or shape God had a clear vision of what it will look like when creation is completed. Vision provides orderliness when it is influenced or backed up by the power of the Holy Spirit. In Genesis 1:2 it is revealed that the Spirit moved upon the waters and then God spoke. Vision is set in motion when we speak.

There are three main questions to answer about vision.

Question #1: Where does vision come from?
Question #2: What do we do with vision?
Question #3: How do we implement the vision?

We'll answer them one after the other.

WHERE DOES VISION COME FROM?

Vision comes from God. We see this in the story of Esau and Jacob.

> *"And the children struggled together within her; and she said, If it be so, why am I thus? And she went to enquire of the Lord. And the Lord said unto her, Two nations are in thy womb, and two manner of people shall be separated from thy bowels; and the one people shall be stronger than the other people; and the elder shall serve the younger." (Genesis 25:22, 23)*

It was already declared before they were born that the elder shall serve the younger, hence, it was easy for Jacob to cheat his brother of his birthright. If you have a vision, commit it to your heart; then it becomes very easy to accelerate the systems to work for you in line with what God has already shown you. Vision will drive you to succeed God's way.

Another example is found in the story of the dreamer, Joseph.

> *"And Joseph dreamed a dream, and he told it his brethren: and they hated him yet the more. And he said unto them, Hear, I pray you, this dream which I have*

> *dreamed: For, behold, we were binding sheaves in the field, and, lo, my sheaf arose, and also stood upright; and, behold, your sheaves stood round about, and made obeisance to my sheaf. And his brethren said to him, Shalt thou indeed reign over us? or shalt thou indeed have dominion over us? And they hated him yet the more for his dreams, and for his words. And he dreamed yet another dream, and told it his brethren, and said, Behold, I have dreamed a dream more; and, behold, the sun and the moon and the eleven stars made obeisance to me." (Genesis 37:5-9)*

From the story of Joseph, we saw that vision could come as a dream. As stated earlier, vision is empowered by words. Joseph gave power to his dream by declaring it, regardless of the risks that were involved in doing so.

Another interesting story along this line is the story of young Mary, the earthly mother of our Lord Jesus Christ.

> *"And the angel answered and said unto her, The Holy Ghost shall come upon thee, and the power of the Highest shall overshadow thee: therefore also that holy thing which shall be born of thee shall be called the Son of God." (Luke 1:35)*

Mary encountered God who revealed yet another vision to her on how He was going to restore man to Himself. Mary also declared the vision, and it was fulfilled as revealed by God to her.

"And Mary said, Behold the handmaid of the Lord; be it unto me according to thy word. And the angel departed from her." (Luke 1:38)

Vision is powerful and can lead the way to a greater and mightier height in life when the Holy Spirit is involved. God has a vision for your life. As Rebecca enquired from the Lord, you, too can ask for the vision for your life.

Food for thought:

> *"Where there is no vision, the people perish: but he that keepeth the law, happy is he." (Proverbs 29:18)*

Destruction is imminent in the absence of vision. To flourish in life, vision must be given its rightful place.

What other ways can vision come? Vision can come by a prophetic utterance. We saw this in the story of Samson:

> *"And the angel of the Lord appeared unto the woman, and said unto her, Behold now, thou art barren, and bearest not: but thou shalt conceive, and bear a son. Now therefore beware, I pray thee, and drink not wine nor strong drink, and eat not any unclean thing: For, lo, thou shalt conceive, and bear a son; and no razor shall come on his head: for the child shall be a Nazarite unto God from the womb: and he shall begin to deliver Israel out of the hand of the Philistines." (Judges 13:3-5)*

Your vision will give you your life mission. God's vision for Samson's life was to deliver the children of Israel from the Philistines. When Samson deviated from that vision, he ended his life in humiliation. A quick lesson to learn here is that when you deviate from your God-given vision, your mission becomes compromised and humiliation looms at the end of the journey.

Another similar example is the prophetic utterance by prophet Isaiah about Jesus Christ:

> *"For unto us a child is born, unto us a son is given: and the government shall be upon his shoulder: and his name shall be called Wonderful, Counsellor, The mighty God, The everlasting Father, The Prince of Peace. Of the increase of his government and peace there shall be no end, upon the throne of David, and upon his kingdom, to order it, and to establish it with judgment and with justice from henceforth even for ever. The zeal of the Lord of hosts will perform this." (Isaiah 9:6-7)*

There is no doubt that the vision statement about Jesus's life became His mission. The vision for our life should only come from God—which brings us to a simple question: Who is speaking prophetically into your life? Someone should have a prophetic voice over your life—and not just anybody. The person could be your minister, father, mother, wife, or your husband.

Finally, on 'where vision comes from'—and this may be the most available source of wisdom to us all—Wisdom comes from the Bible! Yes, many of us will never get a prophetic utterance, might not even dream or hear from God directly, but the Bible will provide each of us with a blueprint that will lead us to our mission in life.

Vision is simply a lamp and light that leads the way, and if vision is indeed a lamp and a light, then vision is The Word!

> *"Thy word is a lamp unto my feet, and a light unto my path." (Psalms 119:105)*

Vision = The Word.

Food for thought:

> *"Wherewithal shall a young man cleanse his way? By taking heed thereto according to thy word." (Psalms 119:9)*

If your vision is going blurry, the only way to revive it is to take it to the Maker and clean it up by the renewal of your mind. The word is powerful enough to do just that.

WHAT DO WE DO WITH THE VISION GOD GIVES US?

Habakkuk gave an answer to this question in his book of visions:

> *"I will stand upon my watch, and set me upon the tower, and will watch to see what he will say unto me, and what I shall answer when I am reproved. And the Lord answered me, and said, write the vision, and make it plain upon tables, that he may run that readeth it." (Habakkuk 2:1-2)*

To receive vision either in your dream, intuition, prophetically or from the word, you will need to be standing upon your watch and be set upon the tower, in a manner of speaking; and when the vision comes, the first thing we do is to **WRITE it down!** To write simply means to execute or produce by setting down words or figures.

The moment you commit a vision to writing, you have given the vision the power to produce or execute. Some of us never take anything serious, let alone writing down anything that can move our life forward. A prudent man or woman is never out of the reach of writing materials at any given time because when you are always on the watch, God can speak or reveal His vision at any moment. Besides, vision is progressive, hence, when we write it down, we can progressively trace the formation of the big picture while also assessing the improvement in the quality of our reception over time.

The second thing we do with vision is to **make it PLAIN.** To make it plain is to make it clear or distinct to the eye or ear, clear to the mind; evident, manifest, or obvious: to make one's sense plain by conveying the meaning clearly and simply; easily understood: plain talk.

When you make your vision plain, it simplifies your life, and allows your vision helpers to locate you easily. We shall expand more on the role of vision helpers in fulfilling your destiny.

It also helps you stick to your appointed time table in prioritizing your activities and involvements in the area of time management. Remember, God created the earth in six days and not in six seconds—which He could have done because He's God. When you make your vision plain, people will not waste your time because your schedule is already laid bare through your plain writings.

The third thing we do with vision is to RUN with it. To run simply means to go quickly by moving more rapidly; to move with haste and act quickly.

Some of us are good at getting our vision, and are disciplined enough to write it down but we are still waiting on God to tell us to go. His instruction is to run with the vision, not even to walk! There is a place of walking in our journey with God (Psalms 1, for example), but in the sphere of vision accomplishment, He said to RUN, which is to move with haste or act quickly. Why? Amongst other reasons, vision takes time to be fulfilled!

Food for thought:

> *"Not slothful in business; fervent in spirit; serving the Lord;" (Romans 12:11).*

To be slothful is to have or show a disposition to avoid exertion; an idle person. Are you slothful? It will be difficult to accomplish anything in idleness.

My prayer for you is that every good word God has spoken concerning you will come to pass this season in Jesus Name.

HOW DO WE IMPLEMENT OUR VISION?

Let us look at the people who ran with the vision they received and how their vision helpers and destroyers influenced the fulfillment of their vision.

May I remind you that because the Lord gives you a vision does not mean it is going to be easy. Remember that the Lord gave the children of Israel the land that is flowing with milk and honey, but there were lots of giants in the land. You might need to displace some giants before you can realize your vision.

There is much to learn about the story of Joseph's vision.

> *"And Joseph dreamed a dream, and he told it his brethren: and they hated him yet the more. And he said unto them, Hear, I pray you, this dream which I have*

> *dreamed: For, behold, we were binding sheaves in the field, and, lo, my sheaf arose, and also stood upright; and, behold, your sheaves stood round about, and made obeisance to my sheaf. And his brethren said to him, Shalt thou indeed reign over us? or shalt thou indeed have dominion over us? And they hated him yet the more for his dreams, and for his words. And he dreamed yet another dream, and told it his brethren, and said, Behold, I have dreamed a dream more; and, behold, the sun and the moon and the eleven stars made obeisance to me." (Genesis 37:5-9)*

The first thing that stood out in this story is that Joseph was able to identify his vision destroyers, but his father set an example for other fathers with regards to their children's vision:

> *"And his brethren envied him; but his father* ***observed*** *the saying." (Genesis 37:11)*

As fathers, our job is to observe and nurture the vision of our children as indicated by their passions and strengths, not to kill it with our words.

1. The fulfillment of any vision begins with an assignment. Sometimes the assignment is as simple as running an errand, changing your location or merely a change in your direction—as indicated in the story of Joseph—and you have to be willing.

> *"And Israel said unto Joseph, Do not thy brethren feed the flock in Shechem? Come, and I will send thee unto them. And he said to him, Here am I." (Genesis 37:13)*

2. Fulfilling your vision will take you an extra mile. But, you cannot quit at the first opportunity to do so. Joseph did not find his brothers at Shechem, yet he went the extra mile, and while he was at it, he met a vision helper that gave him guidance.

The man asked him, "what seeketh thou?" In fact, looking in retrospect, the most appropriate answer he could have given was "I'm looking for my destiny", but guess what? God never gives you the whole details at the beginning of your journey to destiny; as you obey and pass the simple tests, He will bring more clarity to your vision, one step at a time!

> *"And a certain man found him, and, behold, he was wandering in the field: and the man asked him, saying, What seekest thou? And he said, I seek my brethren: tell me, I pray thee, where they feed their flocks. And the man said, They are departed hence; for I heard them say, Let us go to Dothan. And Joseph went after his brethren, and found them in Dothan." (Genesis 37:15-17)*

3. You might find yourself at the opposite end of your vision, or even worse. It might seem that you are off course while your vision destroyers think they have displaced you. They are actually part of the plan to get you to your desired place. What are you going through now? Hang in there, it is all going to come together. There is no coincidence in God's plan for fulfilling your vision. It's okay to desire to have arrived at your destination while you are moving farther away. Even Joseph was sold to a complete stranger, who did not know he had just become a vision helper.

Judas got thirty pieces of silver—what a vision helper he was! I am fully convinced that if he did not kill himself he would have repented and reigned with Jesus in eternity. Do not hate those that are after your vision, their assignment is just for a little moment. The moment Joseph's brothers sold him, their assignment was completed. Thank God for such people in your life, but after all is said and done, a question remains: Do you have passion that it takes to follow through?

> *"And they took him, and cast him into a pit: and the pit was empty, there was no water in it. Then there passed by Midianites merchantmen; and they drew and lifted up Joseph out of the pit, and sold Joseph to the Ishmaelites for twenty pieces of silver: and they brought Joseph into Egypt." (Genesis 37:24, 28)*

> *"And the Midianites sold him into Egypt unto Potiphar, an officer of Pharaoh's, and captain of the guard." (Genesis 37:36)*

Running with the vision might cost you more than you are willing to pay, or keep you longer than you are willing to stay or it might take you farther than you are willing to go, but at the end of it all, it is going to be worth it!

Food for thought:

> *"And we know that all things work together for good to them that love God, to them who are the called according to his purpose." (Romans 8:28)*

If your vision is according to his purpose then everything will work for you. Does your vision align with His purpose? If not go back for clarity to the God who owns the title to your life's vision. Arise and shine for your light is come! This is your moment—seize it and step up to the plate, you are not alone. What an extraordinary life awaits you!

The Lord will like me to tell someone reading this that the assignments He has given you are not moving. Ask yourself, "Am I on the way to fulfilling my assignments?" Another question that the Lord wants me to ask some of you is this, "From whom are you getting your assignments?" Remember, Joseph's assignment came from his Father. If your assignment is not from GOD, THE FATHER then you have missed the mark from the onset and I'm persuaded that the end-result will not be pleasing.

Joseph received his vision in the land of Canaan, but he was sold to the land of Egypt. At that point, he could have given up on the dream, because in his dream his brothers were bowing down to him, but he was sold far away from them such that the literal fulfillment of that vision became no longer feasible in the natural sense.

4. Always remember that it is God's vision for you and not your vision for God. Once you settle that in your heart, I believe you are on your way up to fulfillment.

> *"For my thoughts are not your thoughts, neither are your ways my ways, saith the Lord. For as the heavens are higher than the earth, so are my ways higher than your ways, and my thoughts than your thoughts." (Isaiah 55:8, 9)*

5. Your vision can be fulfilled in such a place where you do not have absolute control over the execution. You are just an actor in a movie that has already been scripted. The further you go in the journey of fulfillment, the more you will need to learn patience.

"And Joseph was brought down to Egypt; and Potiphar, an officer of Pharaoh, captain of the guard, an Egyptian, bought him of the hands of the Ishmaelites, which had brought him down thither." (Genesis 39:1)

Let us examine a second example: David. His fulfillment of his kingship vision began on the battlefield, where he had to battle Goliath—and that was out of his absolute control!

"And Jesse said unto David his son, Take now for thy brethren an ephah of this parched corn, and these ten loaves, and run to the camp to thy brethren; And David rose up early in the morning, and left the sheep with a keeper, and took, and went, as Jesse had commanded him; and he came to the trench, as the host was going forth to the fight, and shouted for the battle...And David spake to the men that stood by him, saying, What shall be done to the man that killeth this Philistine, and taketh away the reproach from Israel? for who is this uncircumcised Philistine, that he should defy the armies of the living God?" (1 Samuel 17:17, 20, 26)

6. Along your journey to fulfillment, you will get to places where you will feel comfortable and things will be working for you, but beware; there are still a lot of battles to be won.

"And the Lord was with Joseph, and he was a prosperous man; and he was in the house of his master the Egyptian. And Joseph found grace in his sight, and he served him: and he made him overseer over his house, and all that

he had he put into his hand." (Genesis 39:2, 4)

Look at David as well:

"Let our lord now command thy servants, which are before thee, to seek out a man, who is a cunning player on an harp: and it shall come to pass, when the evil spirit from God is upon thee, that he shall play with his hand, and thou shalt be well. And Jesse took an ass laden with bread, and a bottle of wine, and a kid, and sent them by David his son unto Saul." (1 Samuel 16:16, 20)

7. You will need to pass some tests before you move to the next level. If you had failed before, grace is available for you today. God has not given up on you, so do not give up on yourself. David came to a point in his journey when he needed to encourage himself in the Lord at Ziklag.

"And it came to pass about this time that Joseph went into the house to do his business; and there was none of the men of the house there within. And she caught him by his garment, saying, Lie with me: and he left his garment in her hand, and fled, and got him out." (Genesis 39:11, 12)

"And David said unto Saul, Thy servant kept his father's sheep, and there came a lion, and a bear, and took a lamb out of the flock: And I went out after him, and smote him, and delivered it out of his mouth: and when he arose against me, I caught him by his beard, and smote him, and slew him." (1 Samuel 17:34, 35)

Food for thought:

> *"Many are the afflictions of the righteous: but the Lord delivereth him out of them all." (Psalms 34:19)*

Are you in a place where you seem to have lost total control? Believe me, I have been there myself. Nevertheless, I am still following Him uncritically because the vision I'm running with is His vision for me and not my vision for Him.

I prophesy into your life and situation today, that every God-inspired vision that has ceased or that are about to die receive divine recovery now in the name of Jesus! From now on, your vision will come alive and come forth as Lazarus came forth out of the tomb.

There are yet more lessons to learn from Joseph's vision. In this strange place where he found himself where he had lost the absolute control of his life, strange things began to happen for the sake of his vision, but because he was well prepared, he navigated through to the land of his fulfillment. We can, as well, for we can do all things through Christ who strengthens us.

Let us look at some new details about Joseph' vision.

8. You must be prepared for setbacks because there will always be more than one on your way to fulfillment. You may ponder, why would God not intervene by preventing the trouble before it ever occurred? After all, Joseph's imprisonment was a complete fabrication from his boss's wife; but you will agree that this is a place where character is being built to prepare him for the large place he would be going. This is the place where patience will have its perfect work so that he might be perfect and lack nothing. This may be applicable to you too, so be prepared:

"And Joseph's master took him, and put him into the prison, a place where the king's prisoners were bound: and he was there in the prison. But the Lord was with Joseph, and shewed him mercy, and gave him favor in the sight of the keeper of the prison." (Genesis 39:20, 21)

Again, we see a parallel in David's life:

"And it came to pass on the morrow, that the evil spirit from God came upon Saul, and he prophesied in the midst of the house: and David played with his hand, as at other times: and there was a javelin in Saul's hand. And Saul cast the javelin; for he said, I will smite David even to the wall with it. And David avoided out of his presence twice." (1 Samuel 18:10, 11)

9. Be productive wherever you find yourself. Do not be limited by any circumstances that you are surrounded by. The fulfillment of your vision is according to God's divine purpose and not that of your own making.

"And the keeper of the prison committed to Joseph's hand all the prisoners that were in the prison; and whatsoever they did there, he was the doer of it. The keeper of the prison looked not to anything that was under his hand; because the Lord was with him, and that which he did, the Lord made it to prosper." (Genesis 39:22, 23)

10. It costs God nothing to cause an uproar in your strange place that will favor you. All you need to know while in the place of waiting is that your time, season and purpose is set by God himself. In the case of Joseph, there was a problem in the palace that would bring him into his place of fulfillment, but for that to happen, he had to activate his God-given gift which worked for him. It is your gift that will bring the fulfillment of your vision. We read the story of the baker and the butler that were imprisoned with Joseph, how they had separate dreams and both were interpreted by Joseph. The butler was restored and the baker was executed according to Joseph's interpretation. That gift paved the way for Joseph.

Your gift can make you stand before kings and not ordinary men. What are you good at? Develop your skills along that line and keep giving expression to it to the best of your ability and you will be on way to the top.

> *"And it came to pass after these things, that the butler of the king of Egypt and his baker had offended their lord the king of Egypt. And he put them in ward in the house of the captain of the guard, into the prison, the place where Joseph was bound." (Genesis 40:1, 3)*

> *"And they said unto him, we have dreamed a dream, and there is no interpreter of it. And Joseph said unto them, do not interpretations belong to God? Tell me them, I pray you." (Genesis 40:8)*

> *"To everything there is a season, and a time to every purpose under the heaven:" (Ecclesiastes 3:1)*

11. Don't put your trust in men—they will forget you. The fulfillment of your dream will not be accomplished by the arm of flesh.

> *"Yet did not the chief butler remember Joseph, but forgat him." (Genesis 40:23)*

Joseph came to his place of fulfillment by demonstrating his gift again. There is no gain saying here; the realization of your vision will come down to how well you keep your gift.

Food for thought:

> *"This matter is by the decree of the watchers, and the demand by the word of the holy ones: to the intent that the living may know that the most High ruleth in the kingdom of men, and giveth it to whomsoever he will, and setteth up over it the basest of men." (Daniel 4:17)*

It is only God that can make a dream from Canaan to be fulfilled in Egypt. He is the beginning and the end of our lives!

12. Your gift will announce your arrival. Joseph's gift brought him up in the discussion when the king had two dreams consecutively. If Joseph was busy complaining in the prison, and remained kept to himself thinking that he did not commit the offense he was serving time for, he would have missed the opportunity to manifest his gift. It doesn't matter how we get to the place of waiting, let us keep our spirit up and serve. The Bible says in all things we should give thanks.

Pharaoh dreamt twice and he needed his dream to be interpreted.

> *"And it came to pass at the end of two full years, that Pharaoh dreamed: and, behold, he stood by the river. And he slept and dreamed the second time: and, behold, seven ears of corn came up upon one stalk, rank and good." (Genesis 41:1, 5)*

13. In the place of your fulfillment, chances are that some people currently are occupying your spot. No wonder, Jesus admonishes us to occupy till He comes (Luke 19:12-13). Some "magicians" and so-called "wise-men" were occupying Joseph's spot. If they were able to interpret the dreams, then Joseph would not be needed and would have remained in prison for some other number of years or so.

The same could be said of David as King Saul was sitting in his rightful place for so many years, and the children of Anakim and the giants were occupying the promised land in Canaan. Today I pray for anything and everything occupying your rightful place to be evacuated in Jesus name, AMEN.

> *"And it came to pass in the morning that his spirit was troubled; and he sent and called for all the magicians of Egypt, and all the wise men thereof: and Pharaoh told them his dream; but there was none that could interpret them unto Pharaoh." (Genesis 41:8)*

14. When the appointed time for the fulfillment of your vision or dream comes, it will be quick, fast and urgent. Remember, "the vision is for an appointed time, that he may run that reads it." When the fulfillment comes, you will need to change some few things. In Joseph's case, he had a shave and changed his garments. I'm persuaded that the Lord will reveal to you what you will need to change to fit in your new position. You cannot say words like "we are like grasshopper in their sight". Your language must also change, and there will be plenty of learning to do.

"Then Pharaoh sent and called Joseph, and they brought him hastily out of the dungeon: and he shaved himself, and changed his raiment, and came in unto Pharaoh." (Genesis 41:14)

"(For we walk by faith, not by sight:)" (2 Corinthians 5:7)

15. You will arrive there. Whatever there is in your vision is by the spirit of God, so that you may know that it is not by your power or might.

"And Pharaoh said unto his servants, Can we find such a one as this is, a man in whom the Spirit of God is?" (Genesis 41:38)

16. God will give you the fulfillment of your vision both literally and exceedingly according to what He had revealed to you. Whatever the Lord has told you, this is your season of fulfillment in Jesus name. Joseph dreamt that his brother bowed to him and it came to pass—not only his brother but citizens of the most powerful nation at that time. In his vision, Joseph saw only his family but God was preparing a nation to bow to him!

"And Pharaoh said unto Joseph, See, I have set thee over all the land of Egypt. And he made him to ride in the second chariot which he had; and they cried before him, BOW THE KNEE: and he made him ruler over all the land of Egypt." (Genesis 41:41, 43)

"And Joseph was the governor over the land, and he it was that sold to all the people of the land: and Joseph's brethren came, and bowed down themselves before him

> *with their faces to the earth. And Joseph remembered the dreams which he dreamed of them, and said unto them, Ye are spies; to see the nakedness of the land ye are come." (Genesis 42:6, 9)*

17. You do not waste time retaliating against the people that directly or indirectly got you to the Promised Land. The most important thing is that you made it to the Promised Land. It also takes time for it to come all together. Joseph dreamt when he was 17, but the vision was not fulfilled until he turned 30. Meaning that it took 13 years in addition to his relocation to another country, for the actualization of his dream.

> *"And Joseph was thirty years old when he stood before Pharaoh king of Egypt. And Joseph went out from the presence of Pharaoh, and went throughout all the land of Egypt." (Genesis 41:46)*

Food for thought:

> *"And he called his ten servants, and delivered them ten pounds, and said unto them, Occupy till I come." (Luke 19:13)*

"Occupy till I come" is a military command. We must not allow the devil to displace us from our place of fulfillment. The devil is like a roaring lion seeking for whom to devour.

CHAPTER 6

FOLLOW THROUGH WITH GOD

> *"Save Caleb the son of Jephunneh the Kenizzite, and Joshua the son of Nun: for they have wholly followed the Lord." (Numbers 32:12)*

Joshua and Caleb went with the spies to Jericho, while the other ten spies gave a bad report about Jericho, they gave a good report because they had another spirit. They wholly followed the Lord. In today's world, we will say that Joshua and Caleb followed through or were highly committed to their cause. To live an extraordinary life, we need to wholly follow the Lord. We cannot follow the Lord half-heartedly or be lukewarm.

> *"I know thy works, that thou art neither cold nor hot: I would thou wert cold or hot. So then because thou art lukewarm, and neither cold nor hot, I will spew thee out of my mouth." (Revelation 3:15, 16)*

This verse started with I KNOW THY WORKS. It is obvious that we cannot hide or deceive God. I am in awe of God, just because He knows us and our situations inside out.

A good example of following God uncritically or wholly even in the presence of danger is the story of the three Hebrews. Greatness does not come without a sacrifice that is sometimes too expensive to pay but with God's grace, nothing is impossible. In the province of Babylon, nobody knows these gentlemen but the story of their lives was about to change because they absolutely followed the Lord.

> *"Nebuchadnezzar the king made an image of gold, whose height was threescore cubits, and the breadth thereof six cubits: he set it up in the plain of Dura, in the province of Babylon. Then an herald cried aloud, To you it is commanded, O people, nations, and languages, That at what time ye hear the sound of the cornet, flute, harp, sackbut, psaltery, dulcimer, and all kinds of musick, ye fall down and worship the golden image that Nebuchadnezzar the king hath set up:" (Daniel 3:1,4,5)*

1. There will always be an opportunity to compromise. Some people had already bowed down to various 'images' in a bid to become great. Have you? Remember, an image is not the real object, but a copy of the original. God is real, all other gods are nothing but a camouflage. If you follow an image, it will lead you nowhere. God is the only way, the truth and the life!

2. There are many voices contesting for your

obedience this day. To whose command are you yielding? The whole nation might be yielding to this worldly commands and pressure, but you should not follow the multitude to do evil. Judges, princes, governors, captains and all the big shots might be doing it, but you must not. To follow absolutely, you must have a spine or will of steel that does not bend!

3. It does not matter who sets the image before you. It does not matter who is giving you commands. It could be your father, mother, husband, wife, boss, friends or children that position themselves as King Nebuchadnezzar in your life —but as long as their command is in opposition to God's commandments, please do not bow.

4. Do not look at the size and magnitude of this image. The image may be big, charming and frightening; it does not matter. It will always be a false evidence appearing real.

5. Do not worship any graven image. Your worship is strictly for the king of kings. Do not worship any graven image because we know that we should have no other gods except JEHOVAH. Your true worship is the only thing God inhabits!

Following God wholly will not always be easy, but more often than none, the way that leads to greatness is narrow and small. Though thy beginning might be small but your latter end shall GREATLY increase.

Food for thought:

> *"Enter ye in at the strait gate: for wide is the gate, and broad is the way, that leadeth to destruction, and many there be which go in there at: Because strait is the gate, and narrow is the way, which leadeth unto life, and few there be that find it." (Matthew 7:13, 14)*

The road—image—to destruction is always wide and huge; be watchful do not be tempted for the devil is around. The story continues…

> *"And whoso falleth not down and worshippeth shall the same hour be cast into the midst of a burning fiery furnace. Therefore at that time, when all the people heard the sound of the cornet, flute, harp, sackbut, psaltery, and all kinds of music, all the people, the nations, and the languages, fell down and worshipped the golden image that Nebuchadnezzar the king had set up." (Daniel 3:6-7)*

6. It is a matter of time. The above Bible verse made a reference to that time, what time? When you will be left to make the decision to either bow or follow the Lord wholly

7. The penalty for not bowing is always sharp. For the 3 Hebrews, the penalty was that they would be thrown into the midst of a burning fiery furnace. I do not know what the cost might be for you whenever you stand for God, but believe me—no price is too much to pay. At the end you will always come out great.

> *"Thou, O king, hast made a decree, that every man that shall hear the sound of the cornet, flute, harp, sackbut,*

psaltery, and dulcimer, and all kinds of musick, shall fall down and worship the golden image:" (Daniel 3:10)

8. When the law of the land is against the law of God, obey the law of God! The king had made a decree! A decree is a strict and imposed order, especially one having the force of law. I am not in any way suggesting that we should break the law, but if it will lead to a compromise of your faith in God, you may need to think twice. You will not be the first or the last one to do so. It is part of God's given wisdom that we discussed earlier in this book.

"There are certain Jews whom thou hast set over the affairs of the province of Babylon, Shadrach, Meshach, and Abed–nego; these men, O king, have not regarded thee: they serve not thy gods, nor worship the golden image which thou hast set up." (Daniel 3:12)

9. People are watching you. The authenticity of your faith is always under the scrutiny of the world. I do not know how big or small Babylon is, but to spot out these 3 Hebrews for not bowing down to a graven image tells me that Christians are constantly being watched through the eyes of the world, ever watching what our reactions will be.

"Now if ye be ready that at what time ye hear the sound of the cornet, flute, harp, sackbut, psaltery, and dulcimer, and all kinds of musick, ye fall down and worship the image which I have made; well: but if ye worship not, ye shall be cast the same hour into the midst of a burning fiery furnace; and who is that God that shall deliver you out of my hands?" (Daniel 3:15)

10. "The king Nebuchadnezzar" in your life will challenge your God. Are you facing any challenge right now telling you "who is that God that shall deliver you out of my hands?" Hey the good news is this: here is what the word says,

> *"Shall the prey be taken from the mighty, or the lawful captive delivered? But thus saith the Lord, Even the captives of the mighty shall be taken away, and the prey of the terrible shall be delivered: for I will contend with him that contendeth with thee, and I will save thy children." (Isaiah 49:24, 25)*

> *Food for thought:*

> *"Whoever does not persevere and carry his own cross and come after" (follow) Me cannot be My disciple." (Luke 14:27 AMP)*

The world is watching your moves. Be a good disciple and make our Lord proud. To follow the Lord exclusively is not always easy but it is very rewarding,

> *"Shadrach, Meshach, and Abednego answered King Nebuchadnezzar, "Your threat means nothing to us. If you throw us in the fire, the God we serve can rescue us from your roaring furnace and anything else you might cook up, O king. But even if he doesn't, it wouldn't make a bit of difference, O king. We still wouldn't serve your gods or worship the gold statue you set up."" (Daniel 3:16-18 MSG)*

11. The enemies' threat should mean nothing to us! Why? Because it gives us the opportunity to exercise our faith and God is a rewarder of those who diligently seek and serve Him. This is where the rubber meets the road; you must believe whether He is or He is not, for you to completely put your trust in Him.

> *"But without faith it is impossible to please him: for he that cometh to God must believe that he is, and that he is a rewarder of them that diligently seek him." (Hebrews 11:6)*

12. You can't sit on the fence. You have to accept or deny God, there is no room for sitting on the fence. Are you ready to trust God even when the result does not go your way? Remember that God makes ALL THINGS beautiful in HIS TIME not on your TIME. The key point is not to bow down to any idol, irrespective of the consequences.

> *"Then was Nebuchadnezzar full of fury, and the form of his visage was changed against Shadrach, Meshach, and Abed–nego: therefore he spake, and commanded that they should heat the furnace one seven times more than it was won't to be heated. And he commanded the most mighty men that were in his army to bind Shadrach, Meshach, and Abed–nego, and to cast them into the burning fiery furnace." (Daniel 3:19-20)*

13. Take a stand for God. When you take a stand for God to live an extraordinary life in God's way, the countenance of the Nebuchadnezzars in your life will change towards you, and then, the Lord will be pleased with you.

The Hebrews are known to constantly pray this prayer (and this is arguably the reason these 3 Hebrews were able to stand):

> *"The Lord make his face shine upon thee, and be gracious unto thee: The Lord lift up his countenance upon thee, and give thee peace." (Numbers 6:25, 26)*

They had God's peace in the face of their danger!

14. The closer you are to your breakthrough, the more the problems you will have to battle. They will intensify just to prove God wrong in your life. For these 3 Hebrews, the furnace was turned up seven times. It was recorded that in the history of that kingdom; the furnace has never been turned up that high. The king had commanded his mighty and strong army to bind these 3 Hebrew men…

> *"Then these men were bound in their coats, their hosen, and their hats, and their other garments, and were cast into the midst of the burning fiery furnace. And these three men, Shadrach, Meshach, and Abed–nego, fell down bound into the midst of the burning fiery furnace." (Daniel 3:21, 23)*

15. God will not stop you from going through the fire. No, He won't, because that is where His deliverance becomes very vivid. I have always wondered why these 3 Hebrews had to go through this ordeal. Can't He just stop it? Yes, He can, but no, He will not. Why? For the same reason He hardened Pharaoh's heart—to show His superiority over him. So whatever you are going through right now that feels like nothing is working, God is about to show up and demonstrate His supremacy.

Food for thought:

> *"For the eyes of the Lord run to and fro throughout the*

whole earth, to shew himself strong in the behalf of them whose heart is perfect toward him." (2 Chronicles 16:9)

His eyes are looking for those who will take a stand for Him. The only way to live an extraordinary life is to live, God's way.

"Then Nebuchadnezzar the king was astonished, and rose up in haste, and spake, and said unto his counsellors, Did not we cast three men bound into the midst of the fire? They answered and said unto the king, True, O king." (Daniel 3:24)

Your own Nebuchadnezzar will also be filled with sudden and overpowering surprise and wonder at the turn of events for good in your life in Jesus name. Your miracle and testimonies will make those ones you denied a bow to rise up and honor you.

"He answered and said, Lo, I see four men loose, walking in the midst of the fire, and they have no hurt; and the form of the fourth is like the Son of God." (Daniel 3:25)

After your ordeal, the God Whom you serve will then become visible for every eye to see. It is in the midst of your fire that you will receive divine visitation. You will also walk without restrictions; nothing shall by any means hurt you. Most importantly, God is with you all through; He is not just visible for every eye to see. He delights to work that way and by so doing, make a fool of the devil. If Satan had known that crucifying Jesus will bring all into the kingdom of God, he would not have done what he did to Jesus. If they saw your fourth dimensions, it will be difficult for you to exercise your faith.

"Then Nebuchadnezzar came near to the mouth of the burning fiery furnace, and spake, and said, Shadrach, Meshach, and Abed–nego, ye servants of the most high God, come forth, and come hither. Then Shadrach, Meshach, and Abed–nego, came forth of the midst of the fire." (Daniel 3:26)

As you strive to lead an extraordinary life by following God absolutely, you will always come forth out of any situation that is meant to destroy you. Remember how Lazarus came forth and was commanded to be released, so shall be your testimony. Because of your testimony, your status will be elevated, from commoners in the palace to the servants of the Most High God.

"And the princes, governors, and captains, and the king's counsellors, being gathered together, saw these men, upon whose bodies the fire had no power, nor was an hair of their head singed, neither were their coats changed, nor the smell of fire had passed on them." (Daniel 3:27)

All those who compromised their significances will gather to celebrate you. That which was intended to kill you will become your lift to an extraordinary life. The fire will not have power over you. As the 3 Hebrews did not lose anything, neither shall you. The fire that was supposed to make you go naked will not have power over your coat, and finally you will miss nothing when you come out; it will be as if you have never gone through that trial or test. The Lord will then restore the years the canker worms and locusts have eaten back to you in many folds.

"Then Nebuchadnezzar spake, and said, Blessed be the God of Shadrach, Meshach, and Abed–nego, who hath

sent his angel, and delivered his servants that trusted in him, and have changed the king's word, and yielded their bodies, that they might not serve nor worship any god, except their own God." (Daniel 3:28)

The image that wants you to bow will end up bowing to your God like king Nebuchadnezzar bowed to the highest God. When you defied the ungodly commands of the king by not yielding your body, and refused to serve their idols, it is only then you will have a firm testimony and will lead an extraordinary life.

"Therefore I make a decree, That every people, nation, and language, which speak anything amiss against the God of Shadrach, Meshach, and Abed–nego, shall be cut in pieces, and their houses shall be made a dunghill: because there is no other God that can deliver after this sort. Then the king promoted Shadrach, Meshach, and Abed–nego, in the province of Babylon." (Daniel 3:29, 30)

The whole saga started with a decree and ended with a decree that brings honor to God. If you do not serve wholly, however, here is what will happen: your life will be cut in pieces and your house will become a dunghill. If you follow God wholly, on the other hand, you will experience unusual deliverance and you will be promoted—a good sign of an extraordinary life.

Food for thought:

"But they that wait upon the Lord shall renew their strength; they shall mount up with wings as eagles; they shall run, and not be weary; and they shall walk, and not faint." (Isaiah 40:31)

An Extraordinary Life

Do you want an extraordinary life? Then wait upon the Lord; it is only then you will mount up with wings as eagles, run and not be weary, and you will walk and not faint. That, my friend, is an extraordinary life.

CHAPTER 7

PRIDE, HAUGHTINESS AND HUMILITY

Praise God for all we have by the blood of Jesus Christ. The foundation for an incredible life is in God. We are seated with Christ in heavenly places far above principalities and powers and we have the "DNA" of Jesus—what an extraordinary life! And talking about the DNA of Jesus, what would that be? HUMILITY!

> *"Let this mind be in you, which was also in Christ Jesus: Who, being in the form of God, thought it not robbery to be equal with God: But made himself of no reputation, and took upon him the form of a servant, and was made in the likeness of men:" (Philippians 2:5-7)*

PRIDE

Pride simply put, is "a high or inordinate opinion of one's own dignity, importance, merit, or superiority, whether as cherished in the mind or as displayed in bearing, or conduct." (dictionary.com, 2016)

"When pride cometh, then cometh shame: but with the lowly is wisdom." (Proverbs 11:2)

"Pride goeth before destruction, and an haughty spirit before a fall." (Proverbs 16:18)

Pride is like a two-tail demon that can come to you or come from you, and the consequences of both dimensions are destructive. On one end; it brings shame and on the other end, it brings destruction. Let's see some examples from the word of God for lessons. Nebuchadnezzar, a great king in the book of Daniel is a good point to start.

Has the scriptures not said that "a man's pride shall bring him low: but honour shall uphold the humble in spirit?" (See Proverbs 29:23). Such was the story of Nebuchadnezzar.

From Daniel 4, we saw that the king himself had a dream about his end and sought out for an adequate interpretation, but he did not to take a good look at his life for a complete inventory of his relationship with man and God. You can read the full story in Daniel 4:1-27.

From his story, we can deduce the following:

1. When there is pride in your life it will be difficult to heed the voice of the Lord. This is the first sign a true follower of Jesus must constantly beware of; when you start making excuses for going your way and not building your life according to the pattern shown by the word, there is a big trouble!

"The wicked, through the pride of his countenance, will not seek after God: God is not in all his thoughts." (Psalms 10:4)

"All this came upon the king Nebuchadnezzar. At the end of twelve months he walked in the palace of the kingdom of Babylon. The king spake, and said, Is not this great Babylon, that I have built for the house of the kingdom by the might of my power, and for the honour of my majesty?" (Daniel 4:28-30)

2. Don't forget the source of your strength. Beware when you take a complete inventory of what you have or what you've acquired, not forgetting that it is not by your power or might but by God's spirit. Who do you give credit for your success to? Yourself or GOD? A big question that can only be answered by you.

At the end of twelve months—which is symbolic of the end of the year—the king walked in the palace. Who receives credit for keeping you till the year end? God is the Alpha and Omega, the beginning and the end. Anybody who wants to play that role out of pride will fall awfully. Every opportunity to start or end anything or any project, should be ascribed to God because that is His moment. He owns the beginning and the end of every second, minute, hour, day, week, month and year and we should not attempt to occupy that position in His stead.

"So teach us to number our days, that we may apply our hearts unto wisdom." (Psalms 90:12)

"While the word was in the king's mouth, there fell a voice from heaven, saying, O king Nebuchadnezzar, to thee it is spoken; The kingdom is departed from thee." (Daniel 4:31 KJV)

3. God has made us kings and priests unto himself. There is a prominent phrase in the story: "while the word was still in the king's mouth..." Amongst other things, the phrase brings up a link between kings and words... and as kings and priests, we have the capacity to use words as well.

> *"And hath made us kings and priests unto God and his Father; to him be glory and dominion for ever and ever. Amen." (Revelation 1:6)*

As a king what kind of word is coming from your mouth? What is the meditation of your heart? It will determine what kind of voice that will come from heaven to you. Is it going to be that of judgement or of favor? Check your heart if pride has crept in.

> *"Keep thy heart with all diligence; for out of it are the issues of life." (Proverbs 4:23)*

4. Pride can rob you of 'your kingdom'. "The kingdom is the departed from thee." Has your kingdom departed from you because of PRIDE? It is very possible while the love of God towards you can prevent judgement because of his finished work, less you might lose your kingdom. The prodigal son, out of pride and self-indulgence, acted out what was on his mind and the word of his mouth led him in the path of destruction. The ethics of this story is that, as the prodigal son walked away from the kingdom, it is very possible to lose your kingdom—your sphere of influence—as well because of pride.

Food for thought:

> *"And I will break the pride of your power; and I will make your heaven as iron, and your earth as brass:" (Leviticus 26:19)*

Do you want your heaven to be as iron or your earth to be as brass? What are you going to choose? LIFE OR DEATH.

> *"I call heaven and earth to record this day against you, that I have set before you; life and death, blessing and cursing: therefore choose life, that both thou and thy seed may live:" (Deuteronomy 30:19)*

5. God still rules in the affairs of men! What a thought that God is still very much interested in our affairs as consistently as we let him in! God is perfectly gentle—He will not come in when He's not invited. Behold He is standing at the door of your heart waiting for invitation. This isn't just true for someone who is yet to accept Christ as his personal Lord and Savior but also for every decision we make, He is waiting for us to ask of His opinion. Only the proud will not care of Jesus's opinion on the matters of his/her life.

> *"And they shall drive thee from men, and thy dwelling shall be with the beasts of the field: they shall make thee to eat grass as oxen, and seven times shall pass over thee, until thou know that the most High ruleth in the kingdom of men, and giveth it to whomsoever he will. The same hour was the thing fulfilled upon Nebuchadnezzar: and he was driven from men, and did eat grass as oxen, and his body was wet with the dew of heaven, till his hairs were grown like eagles' feathers, and his nails like birds' claws." (Daniel 4:32-33)*

What a terrible effect pride has! It will drive you away from men. Take a closer look at your surroundings, are you living among men? Or has your pride driven good and valuable allies away from you?

Are you not dwelling among the 'beasts of the field'? Take a complete inventory of your associates, are they of beastly nature? What kind of association are you into? When pride drives good people away, they will be replaced by beasts—there is no room for vacuum. Are you the brightest and smartest in your circle of friends? You might need to move out and begin to learn again.

> *"They shall make you eat grass as oxen".*

When you lose touch with 'humans' and take to dwelling among beasts, you will start doing 'beastly' things like eating grass (in a manner of speaking). Talk of having an affair outside of your marriage, stealing, cheating others, etc; you find yourself allowing things that you wouldn't even consider before. Pride will bring you very low and take you in the opposite direction of an extraordinary life.

More so, pride will change your outlook! Learn from Nebuchadnezzar; his body was wet with the dew of heaven, till his hairs were grown like eagles' feathers, and his nails like birds' claws. Pride will make you ugly, and it will destroy your reputation.

> *"And at the end of the days I Nebuchadnezzar lifted up mine eyes unto heaven, and mine understanding returned unto me, and I blessed the most High, and I praised and honoured him that liveth for ever, whose dominion is an everlasting dominion, and his kingdom is from generation to generation:" (Daniel 4:34)*

Pride will take your understanding away, but the Lord will

restore your understanding the moment you lift up your eyes and acknowledge Him. Are you in need of understating? Please humble yourself and the Lord will restore what the locusts and the canker worms had eaten.

> *"And even as they did not like to retain God in their knowledge, God gave them over to a reprobate mind, to do those things which are not convenient;" (Romans 1:28)*

Food for thought:

> *"At the same time my reason returned unto me; and for the glory of my kingdom, mine honor and brightness returned unto me; and my counsellors and my lords sought unto me; and I was established in my kingdom, and excellent majesty was added unto me. Now I Nebuchadnezzar praise and extol and honor the King of heaven, all whose works are truth, and his ways judgment: and those that walk in pride he is able to abase." (Daniel 4:36, 37)*

Full restoration awaits you if only you can adopt the "DNA of Jesus Christ" which is "HUMILITY".

Pride is so dangerous and terribly poisonous that it can become generational if it is not dealt with effectively. Looking at the life and the family of king Nebuchadnezzar, it became obvious that pride also destroyed his son king Belshazzar. Despite witnessing his father's pride-induced exile, he manifested the same vice. It's obvious that he inherited that behavior from his father. He must have seen how his father treated his palace servants, wives and lords.

Like father, like son; here is the story of King Belshazzar's life:

> *"Belshazzar the king made a great feast to a thousand of his lords, and drank wine before the thousand. Belshazzar, whiles he tasted the wine, commanded to bring the golden and silver vessels which his father Nebuchadnezzar had taken out of the temple which was in Jerusalem; that the king, and his princes, his wives, and his concubines, might drink therein. Then they brought the golden vessels that were taken out of the temple of the house of God which was at Jerusalem; and the king, and his princes, his wives, and his concubines, drank in them." (Daniel 5:1-3)*

Please endeavor to make amends when you realize that you have done something wrong, especially as a result of your pride. Belshazzar's father took out the vessels from the house of the Lord but never returned them even after he repented and was restored. He left a snare in his own house that became a problem for his son. "Restitution is the restoration of property or rights previously taken away, conveyed or surrendered, also a restoration to the former or original state or position". (thefreedictionary.com, 2016)

What are the things that belong to God that you are keeping in your house? Remember, one of the definitions of pride is "becoming or having a dignified sense of what is due to oneself". From this definition, therefore, it is obvious that it is pride that makes you rob God of your tithe and offerings or make you outrightly steal from the church's treasury, because pride tells you it belongs to you, whereas, it will only become a snare.

> *"They drank wine, and praised the gods of gold, and of silver, of brass, of iron, of wood, and of stone." (Daniel 5:4)*

When you take what does not belong to you (which your pride excuses you to claim as yours), you tend to use it the wrong way and for wrong reasons. The king drank from the vessel and began to praise the god of gold, silver, brass, iron, wood and of stone. The time you are supposed to be in the presence of God, pride tells you that it is your free time. What do you use those time for? Nothing productive! The tithe and offerings you took from the house of the Lord, How did you spend the money? And on what did you spend the money? You are the only one that can answer those questions. He who steals God's money is the architect of his own misfortune!

> *"In the same hour came forth fingers of a man's hand, and wrote over against the candlestick upon the plaster of the wall of the king's palace: and the king saw the part of the hand that wrote. Then the king's countenance was changed, and his thoughts troubled him, so that the joints of his loins were loosed, and his knees smote one against another." (Daniel 5:5, 6)*

What is the finger of the Lord writing to you because of your pride? Are you going to take a time out? Has your countenance changed because of the word from the Lord to you? Are you afraid of the consequences of your pride? You are the only one that can answer these questions.

> *"O thou king, the most high God gave Nebuchadnezzar thy father a kingdom, and majesty, and glory, and honour: And for the majesty that he gave him, all people,*

> *nations, and languages, trembled and feared before him: whom he would he slew; and whom he would he kept alive; and whom he would he set up; and whom he would he put down. But when his heart was lifted up, and his mind hardened in pride, he was deposed from his kingly throne, and they took his glory from him: And he was driven from the sons of men; and his heart was made like the beasts, and his dwelling was with the wild asses: they fed him with grass like oxen, and his body was wet with the dew of heaven; till he knew that the most high God ruled in the kingdom of men, and that he appointeth over it whomsoever he will. And thou his son, O Belshazzar, hast not humbled thine heart, though thou knewest all this; But hast lifted up thyself against the Lord of heaven; and they have brought the vessels of his house before thee, and thou, and thy lords, thy wives, and thy concubines, have drunk wine in them; and thou hast praised the gods of silver, and gold, of brass, iron, wood, and stone, which see not, nor hear, nor know: and the God in whose hand thy breath is, and whose are all thy ways, hast thou not glorified:" (Daniel 5:18-23)*

Like father like son, what legacy are you leaving for your children?

> *"O thou king, the most high God gave Nebuchadnezzar thy father a kingdom, and majesty, and glory, and honour: Then was the part of the hand sent from him; and this writing was written. And this is the writing that was written, MENE, MENE, TEKEL, UPHARSIN. This is the interpretation of the thing: MENE; God hath numbered thy kingdom, and finished it. TEKEL; Thou art weighed in the balances, and art*

> *found wanting. PERES; Thy kingdom is divided, and given to the Medes and Persians. In that night was Belshazzar the king of the Chaldeans slain." (Daniel 5:18, 24-28, 30)*

At the end of the day, the proud will come to a sudden end, because God has numbered their kingdoms and they are concluded. They are found defective because they will always come short and their kingdoms are divided and will be given to those who are humble. God is still in the business of having seven available replacements at any given time for his chosen ones.

Food for thought:

> *"A seed shall serve him; it shall be accounted to the Lord for a generation." (Psalms 22:30)*

The same goes for the proud, he can destroy an entire generation because of his pride; please beware. The legacy we leave for our children, followers, or coworkers is of utmost importance, Paul said we should be careful what we build on the foundation of Christ because everyone's work will be tried and tested by fire. May your works stand the test!

In staying true to our focus on how to continue to enjoy the extraordinary life that Christ has won for us, there is another vice that we must watch out for. This shall be discussed next:

HAUGHTINESS

To be haughty is to be "disdainfully proud, snobbish, scornfully arrogant, and supercilious". (dictionary.com, 2016)

"Before destruction the heart of man is haughty, and before honour is humility." (Proverbs 18:12)

When you see that you are becoming snobbish, a little bit of arrogance setting in or you are beginning to treat people with contempt, know that you are heading for destruction. This malady always begin in the heart. Lucifer, the ex-morning star and an ex-arch-angel, threaded that path and will eternally regret doing so. The word of God gives us the record:

"How art thou fallen from heaven, O Lucifer, son of the morning! How art thou cut down to the ground, which didst weaken the nations!" (Isaiah 14:12)

Note the three-letter word repeated twice in that verse of the scripture, "HOW". How do you fall from where you are to the base? The one word answer is 'haughtiness'. Haughtiness will bring you down. It manifests when you become so ambitious that it does not matter how you get to the top. Beware of such a trait; it is very deadly. It will readily deprive you of an extraordinary life.

"For thou hast said in thine heart, I will ascend into heaven, I will exalt my throne above the stars of God: I will sit also upon the mount of the congregation, in the sides of the north: I will ascend above the heights of the clouds; I will be like the most High." (Isaiah 14:13, 14)

This is the usual pathway: It always begins in your heart when nobody sees it; it is only between you and God. Nothing is wrong with having an ambition—an earnest desire for some type of achievement or distinction, as power, honor and fame—that is good but when you want to displace somebody with every means necessary it becomes evil, and it becomes haughtiness.

> *"Yet thou shalt be brought down to hell, to the sides of the pit. They that see thee shall narrowly look upon thee, and consider thee, saying, Is this the man that made the earth to tremble, that did shake kingdoms; That made the world as a wilderness, and destroyed the cities thereof; that opened not the house of his prisoners?" (Isaiah 14:15-17)*

The end result is fatal! Instead of an extraordinary life, it leads to hell and shame. Instead of gaining, it end in a big loss. You will lose your place, isolated and completely dejected. Please remain humble always and it shall be well with you and you shall mount up with wings as eagle effortlessly.

> *"And upon a set day Herod, arrayed in royal apparel, sat upon his throne, and made an oration unto them. And the people gave a shout, saying, It is the voice of a god, and not of a man. And immediately the angel of the Lord smote him, because he gave not God the glory: and he was eaten of worms, and gave up the ghost. But the word of God grew and multiplied." (Acts 12:21-24)*

Take a look at King Herod and learn a lesson or two. From his story, we discover that the people surrounding you may make you haughty without you knowing it. It is very dangerous when you bask in the praise of men instead of giving all glory unto God. Are you dead inside—certainly, there are many walking-dead on the earth now because of haughtiness. Are you one of them? May God have mercy on you, as you turn to Him, amen.

When King Herod died the word of God grew; that is a simple proof that any man that will not submit to God will be taken out of the way. For God to show you that you are replaceable, He will make his word grow while you are out of the picture. Beware of haughtiness, you don't want to be robbing shoulder with your Maker.

Food for thought:

> *"The lofty looks of man shall be humbled, and the haughtiness of men shall be bowed down, and the Lord alone shall be exalted in that day. For the day of the Lord of hosts shall be upon every one that is proud and lofty, and upon every one that is lifted up; and he shall be brought low:" (Isaiah 2:11, 12)*

When you are proud and haughty you set yourself against GOD, so ask yourself, "Can I handle that?"

HUMILITY

Living with humility will help you to put a lot of things in perspective and bring many decisions in your life to line up with the word of God. God will not change His word to fit your situation, you must get your ways to line up with His counsel for your life. We cannot be conformed to the world, rather we must be transformed by the renewing of our mind. Are you seeking to know the will of God? Then you must renew your mind. An extraordinary life is the will of God for us.

> *"And be not conformed to this world: but be ye transformed by the renewing of your mind, that ye may prove what is that good, and acceptable, and perfect, will of God." (Romans 12:2)*

Humility is not to be mistaken for weakness, rather it makes you a winner. It gives you more than you can ever ask for. The simple way to look at this attribute is to study people who possess that virtue. Let us look at the story of Solomon. Remember Solomon was born to a man who killed his mother's ex-husband and to a woman who committed adultery. But God blessed him greatly despite the history trailing his background. Why?

> *"In Gibeon the Lord appeared to Solomon in a dream by night: and God said, Ask what I shall give thee." (1 Kings 3:5)*

For starters, he wasn't greedy. Greedy people are not humble people! Greed is indirectly related to humility. Greed is an excessive or limitless desire especially for wealth or possessions. The greedy seeks selfish ways to get to the top while the humble delights in making the lives of the people around him or her better, as a result such individual not only gets to the top but speeds-up to the top; which is the result a greedy person is actively seeking.

> *"And Solomon said, Thou hast shewed unto thy servant David my father great mercy, according as he walked before thee in truth, and in righteousness, and in uprightness of heart with thee; and thou hast kept for him this great kindness, that thou hast given him a son to sit on his throne, as it is this day." (1 Kings 3:6)*

Humility will make you take a good inventory of what God has done for you and your family as a whole. Humility will make you thank God for keeping you and your family in the path of righteousness and not having the sense of entitlement of any sort.

> *"And now, O Lord my God, thou hast made thy servant king instead of David my father: and I am but a little child: I know not how to go out or come in. And thy servant is in the midst of thy people which thou hast chosen, a great people, that cannot be numbered nor counted for multitude." (1 Kings 3:7, 8)*

Humility will make you look inside. King David danced to God half-naked because he understood that he was before the King of kings, and in acknowledgement of his helplessness. Humility will give you adequate assessment of your strengths and weaknesses, and will help you to ask for the right thing.

> *"Give therefore thy servant an understanding heart to judge thy people, that I may discern between good and bad: for who is able to judge this thy so great a people?" (1 Kings 3:9)*

Humility will put everything in the right perspective for you. It will guide you to ask for the right thing, as well as help you to distinguish between good and bad. Humility will give you a great understanding of the situation at hand.

> *"And the speech pleased the Lord, that Solomon had asked this thing. And God said unto him, Because thou hast asked this thing, and hast not asked for thyself long life; neither hast asked riches for thyself, nor hast asked the life of thine enemies; but hast asked for thyself understanding to discern judgment;" (1 Kings 3:10, 11)*

When was the last time your speech pleased the Lord? David must have done a good job teaching his son – Solomon about our great God. Remember that David said "I have been young, and now am old; yet have I not seen the righteous forsaken, nor his seed begging bread". (Psalm 37:25) What are you teaching your kids?

When you pray what are you really asking for us? Back in my home country, Nigeria, you will see us as believers asking God in prayers that our enemies should fall and die without repentance; we ask for riches and can even fast for 21 days so that we can outlive our enemies even when we are not productive. God is obviously not happy when we constantly ask for that.

> *"Behold, I have done according to thy words: lo, I have given thee a wise and an understanding heart; so that there was none like thee before thee, neither after thee shall any arise like unto thee. And I have also given thee that which thou hast not asked, both riches, and honour: so that there shall not be any among the kings like unto thee all thy days." (1 Kings 3:12, 13)*

"The result of humility will always exceed your expectation, one, God will answer that question and then give you an extraordinary answer. God said I will break this mode after this nobody will ever be as you. If we can value Solomon's worth in today's economy I am sure he will be far ahead of the richest man right now which is Jeff Bezos 130.3 Billion USD" (Bill Gates).

Food for thought:

> *"Wisdom is the principal thing; therefore get wisdom: and with all thy getting get understanding." (Proverbs 4:7)*

What did Solomon ask for? An understanding heart! Take that as a word of advice; when you are in need of direction, always ask for an understanding heart for the situation at hand, instead of a quick fix answer for that problem. That will get you a solution of a lifetime!

Hallelujah! Jesus has overcome all our problems by His finished work on the cross. What an example Jesus is for us, if we study His life! He can be described as the embodiment of humility. The Bible says "he humbled himself even unto death". Jesus is the author of an extraordinary life.

We can learn a lot from Jesus regarding humility starting from His birth to His death and resurrection.

- **His birth:**
  "And, behold, thou shalt conceive in thy womb, and bring forth a son, and shalt call his name JESUS. He shall be great, and shall be called the Son of the Highest: and the Lord God shall give unto him the throne of his father David: And he shall reign over the house of Jacob forever; and of his kingdom there shall be no end." (Luke 1:31-33)

Nobody in human history has ever had this type of divine visitation [in the natural form], that resulted in a birth without the union of a man and a woman. What an outstanding birth story! If it were to be you and me, nobody will be able to approach us, let alone talking to us or seeing us walk among the people. What a lesson for the so-called men and women of God that suddenly turned unapproachable because of the few miraculous signs wrought in their ministry.

"He shall be great, shall be called the son of the highest, the Lord shall give him the throne of David and reign over the house of Jacob forever, and of his kingdom there shall be no end". What a promise and pronouncement! Yet, He was found among the poor, destitute, and often in the foxhole during His time here on earth. Are you high and mighty because of the word the Lord has spoken to you or because of what the Lord is doing with you? Please put on humility so that you can go further in your walk with the master.

- **His Profession**
  "Is not this the Carpenter's son? Is not his mother called Mary? And his brethren, James, and Joses, and Simon, and Judas?" (Matthew 13:55)

The son of a carpenter. History had it that he did help his father in that profession, and practiced the same till about age 30 when He started public ministry. He was actively involved in His father's (Joseph's) business. That's a news flash to those who have a problem identifying with their family let alone helping them out. Some cannot submit to their parent because they believe that they are 'called'. Are you too big for others? Or, worse still, are you too big for the God that called or saved you? "Humility is Jesus's DNA", so examine your "chromosome".

- **His Ministry**
  "And when he was come into his own country, he taught them in their synagogue, insomuch that they were astonished, and said, Whence hath this man this wisdom, and these mighty works? And they were offended in him. But Jesus said unto them, A prophet is not without honour, save in his own country, and in his own house. And he did not many mighty works there because of their unbelief." (Matthew 13:54, 57-58)

So many miracles, mighty works and great demonstrations of godly wisdom! In today's world, Jesus would be a superstar in His hometown, but in His days, He could not even do much work in His own town; He was not a superstar nor a celebrity. What a lesson from the biggest superstar ever to walk this planet! What an epitome of humility. A great lesson for all of us.

- **His Death**

  "Who, being in the form of God, thought it not robbery to be equal with God: But made himself of no reputation, and took upon him the form of a servant, and was made in the likeness of men: And being found in fashion as a man, he humbled himself, and became obedient unto death, even the death of the cross." (Philippians 2:6-8)

What a faithful servant! He followed His orders to the end. He does not see Himself as being equal to God though He is the second person in the Godhead, He made himself of no reputation—He had nothing to protect. He did not ask, 'why Me?', He humbled Himself unto death. What a man! Men's man! I will like to be like Him. What about you?

- **His Resurrection**

  "And, behold, there was a great earthquake: for the angel of the Lord descended from heaven, and came and rolled back the stone from the door, and sat upon it. He is not here: for he is risen, as he said. Come, see the place where the Lord lay." (Matthew 28:2, 6)

One would have thought that after the resurrection He would switch to a superstar status. But not even His disciples were able to recognize Him nor accorded Him such status. If it were you, won't there be sirens and all sorts of trumpets blowing announcing your whereabouts with a press coverage at every event you attend. No, not Jesus! Rather, He made sure the disciples did not miss focus on the tasks ahead. He gathered them to Jerusalem to receive the promised Holy Ghost.

- **His Reward**

> *"Wherefore God also hath highly exalted him, and given him a name which is above every name: That at the name of Jesus every knee should bow, of things in heaven, and things in earth, and things under the earth; And that every tongue should confess that Jesus Christ is Lord, to the glory of God the Father." (Philippians 2:9-11)*

Do you want an exceedingly extraordinary life? Jesus is our perfect example of how to achieve that, and the only way He laid as an example for us to follow is through humility. It should be our cloak and our identity. God will exalt and lift you up like He did Jesus.

Food for thought:

> *"By humility and the fear of the Lord are riches, and honour, and life." (Proverbs 22:4)*

Some of the evidence of an extraordinary life is to have riches and to be honored among our peers, community or church; it all comes from humility.

CHAPTER 8

HIGH PRAISE AND WORSHIP

Praise and worship is such a vital part of our life that in many houses of worship, praising and singing always precede all services. Why? This is because we believe that it ushers in the presence of God and also that it is the only weapon that moves the hand of God on behalf of the praise worshippers. We have numerous examples in the Bible to back that up.

Another important thing about worship is that it is basically the only thing done in heaven! All day long, there is never a break in praising God. No wonder there are no problems in heaven, no sicknesses, no lack, no death, no pestilence, no terrorist attack, in short; it is all peaceful.

Let us look at this Bible verse:

> *"Thy kingdom come. Thy will be done in earth, as it is in heaven." (Matthew 6:10)*

This is Jesus teaching us to pray and one of the powerful lines in that prayer aims at bringing down or establishing the kingdom of God, and for the will of God to be done on earth as it is in heaven. How do we do that? It can only be established through praise and worship.

Let us look at the classical story of king Jehoshaphat:

> *"It came to pass after this also, that the children of Moab, and the children of Ammon, and with them other beside the Ammonites, came against Jehoshaphat to battle. Then there came some that told Jehoshaphat, saying, There cometh a great multitude against thee from beyond the sea on this side Syria; and, behold, they be in Hazazon–tamar, which is En–gedi. And Jehoshaphat feared, and set himself to seek the Lord, and proclaimed a fast throughout all Judah." (2 Chronicles 20:1-3)*

For you to be able to use this weapon called praise and worship, be rest assured that the devil will attack you. Know this also that because the demons understand the power you have through praise and worship, they will come in a great multitude against you. Their target is to battle against your health, finances, family, job, business, and most importantly your faith, so be prepared to engage.

> *"And Jehoshaphat feared, and set himself to seek the Lord, and proclaimed a fast throughout all Judah".*

Humanly speaking, it is natural to be afraid when we get overwhelmed, but it is not okay to stay afraid. Instead of running around like a chicken with no head, we should set ourselves apart to seek the Lord with our household and engage the most powerful weapon of praise and worship.

> *"And Jehoshaphat stood in the congregation of Judah*

> *and Jerusalem, in the house of the Lord, before the new court, and said, O Lord God of our fathers, art not thou God in heaven? And rulest not thou over all the kingdoms of the heathen? And in thine hand is there not power and might, so that none is able to withstand thee? Art not thou our God, who didst drive out the inhabitants of this land before thy people Israel, and gavest it to the seed of Abraham thy friend forever? And they dwelt therein, and have built thee a sanctuary therein for thy name, saying," (2 Chronicles 20:5-8)*

Let us learn from King Jehoshaphat, to pray back to God His own Word. God is moved when we take Him at His word. He said heaven and earth shall pass away, but His Word will abide forever. Remind Him of the past victories that He has given you, not that the Lord forgets but just to show your appreciation to Him for His goodness.

> *"Behold, I say, how they reward us, to come to cast us out of thy possession, which thou hast given us to inherit. O our God, wilt thou not judge them? for we have no might against this great company that cometh against us; neither know we what to do: but our eyes are upon thee." (2 Chronicles 20:11, 12)*

Be sure of your inheritance. Sickness, lack, or stagnant business is not your portion. Re-establish yourself in your inheritance and get to understand what God has given you. You are not trying to get it, it is already given to you by the finished work of Jesus Christ.

It is not for you to judge your adversaries, if you do that you will limit the amount of victories God is going to get for you. King Jehoshaphat asked God to Judge his enemies.

He acknowledged his lack of might needed to face the situation, so he let go and let God help him.

Food for thought:

> *"But thou art holy, O thou that inhabitest the praises of Israel." (Psalms 22:3)*

Do you want to see God in action on your behalf, then engage Him in worship and your life will be filled with His glory. You are on your way to an extraordinary life. God bless you and your household as you praise and worship him.

> *"And all Judah stood before the Lord, with their little ones, their wives, and their children. Then upon Jahaziel the son of Zechariah, the son of Benaiah, the son of Jeiel, the son of Mattaniah, a Levite of the sons of Asaph, came the Spirit of the Lord in the midst of the congregation;" (2 Chronicles 20:13, 14)*

Whatever you are going through, please stay in God's presence like all Judah did until the spirit of the Lord moved. When the spirit moved, God's instructions of deliverance began to flow like water.

> *"And he said, Hearken ye, all Judah, and ye inhabitants of Jerusalem, and thou king Jehoshaphat, Thus saith the Lord unto you, Be not afraid nor dismayed by reason of this great multitude; for the battle is not yours, but God's." (2 Chronicles 20:15)*

Consequently, we start preparing for the next phase of our life with this word as we praise and worship Him. God will begin to speak to you for your next season as you praise and worship Him.

"Do not be afraid nor dismayed by reason of this great multitude…"--Emotional problems, financial, kids in trouble, failure in business, lack of steady employment, unstable health—whatever the problem may be, He is saying to you, "be not afraid, no fear in your future."

"For the battle is not yours, but God's." Wait and see the salvation of the Lord. It is God's time to fight for you; it is your time to praise and worship His name! Maybe you think that you do not have anything to praise and worship God about, but remember that we walk by faith and not by sight.

> *"Tomorrow go ye down against them: behold, they come up by the cliff of Ziz; and ye shall find them at the end of the brook, before the wilderness of Jeruel. Ye shall not need to fight in this battle: set yourselves, stand ye still, and see the salvation of the Lord with you, O Judah and Jerusalem: fear not, nor be dismayed; tomorrow go out against them: for the Lord will be with you." (2 Chronicles 20:16, 17)*

"…tomorrow…" I declare unto you that tomorrow literarily starts your new day of victory in the name of Jesus. You may have been in need up till now, but tomorrow marks the beginning of a new season for you in the name of Jesus.

In learning from Jehoshaphat, below are the instructions followed to the letter:

- You need not to fight in this battle,
- Set yourself to worship and praise the Lord,
- Stand ye still and stop all activities; stop trying to help God,

- See your salvation in your next season, and receive deliverance from all your troubles for the Lord will be with you.

"And Jehoshaphat bowed his head with his face to the ground: and all Judah and the inhabitants of Jerusalem fell before the Lord, worshipping the Lord. And the Levites, of the children of the Kohathites, and of the children of the Kohathites, stood up to praise the Lord God of Israel with a loud voice on high. And they rose early in the morning, and went forth into the wilderness of Tekoa: and as they went forth, Jehoshaphat stood and said, Hear me, O Judah, and ye inhabitants of Jerusalem; Believe in the Lord your God, so shall ye be established; believe his prophets, so shall ye prosper." (2 Chronicles 20:18-20)

As God's prophet today, I am declaring His word of victory into your next season. You are blessed! You shall prosper!

"And when he had consulted with the people, he appointed singers unto the Lord, and that should praise the beauty of holiness, as they went out before the army, and to say, Praise the Lord; for his mercy endureth for ever. And when they began to sing and to praise, the Lord set ambushments against the children of Ammon, Moab, and mount Seir, which were come against Judah; and they were smitten." (2 Chronicles 20:21, 22)

That is how we get the victory. Begin to praise God for who He is, and for the beauty of His holiness; praise Him with your voice, and hands. Then the Lord will set ambushments against the enemies of your progress.

To set an ambush is an act or instance of attacking unexpectedly from a concealed position. Your trouble days are over because God is attacking those problems from a concealed position.

Food for thought:

> *"Out of the mouth of babes and sucklings hast thou ordained strength because of thine enemies, that thou mightest still the enemy and the avenger." (Psalms 8:2)*

If you want God to still your enemies and the avengers then you must engage the weapon of radical praise and worship. If you need strength to do this, please praise for it. Praise him like a baby. "Let everything that hath breath praise the Lord."

Having seen what God did for King Jehoshaphat in the Old Testament, let us look at God's goodness birthed from the womb of praise in the New Testament:

> *"And it came to pass, as we went to prayer, a certain damsel possessed with a spirit of divination met us, which brought her masters much gain by soothsaying: The same followed Paul and us, and cried, saying, These men are the servants of the most high God, which shew unto us the way of salvation. And this did she many days. But Paul, being grieved, turned and said to the spirit, I command thee in the name of Jesus Christ to come out of her. And he came out the same hour. And when her masters saw that the hope of their gains was gone, they caught Paul and Silas, and drew them into the marketplace unto the rulers," (Acts 16:16-19)*

Let me congratulate you, because I believe that the problem you have been struggling with comes to an end in the name of Jesus. This problem of demonic divination had followed Paul and Silas for many days, but it all came to an end one fateful day. I decree that every spirit of divination that has been following you about and which has prospered against you in the time past till now comes to an end today in the name of Jesus. Why? Because all the prayers that you have been praying has been answered. As a result of this victory, remember that the devil does not take defeat lightly, please do not let down your guard. Let us learn from Paul and Silas.

As he did for them, the devil—the accuser of the brethren—will bring your case up and will try to persecute you. When that time comes, just remember your greatest weapons: praise and worship.

> *"And brought them to the magistrates, saying, these men, being Jews, do exceedingly trouble our city, And teach customs, which are not lawful for us to receive, neither to observe, being Romans. And the multitude rose up together against them: and the magistrates rent off their clothes, and commanded to beat them." (Acts 16:20-22)*

As they rose against Paul and Silas, multitude will rise against you to do all they can, but I pray for you that every lie that the devil has told about you shall be defeated by the power in the blood and the finished work of Jesus Christ, Amen.

> *"And when they had laid many stripes upon them, they cast them into prison, charging the jailor to keep them safely: Who, having received such a charge, thrust them into the inner prison, and made their feet fast in the stocks." (Acts 16:23, 24)*

That was the devil's worst, but as God delivered Paul and Silas, so shall God set you free from any kind of prison you might have been, be it sickness, financial lack, unsteady employment, difficult boss, troubled kid, troubled home, having difficulty becoming pregnant, whatsoever it may be, you are coming out now, in Jesus name, Amen!

> *"And at midnight Paul and Silas prayed, and sang praises unto God: and the prisoners heard them. And suddenly there was a great earthquake, so that the foundations of the prison were shaken: and immediately all the doors were opened, and every one's bands were loosed." (Acts 16:25, 26)*

"At midnight…" Praise God, this is your midnight hour to pray and sing praises unto Him. You are not only coming out, you are bringing every prisoner in your family, work place, your church, and neighborhood with you in Jesus name, Amen.

". . . suddenly…a great earthquake…" There are two interesting words in the verse above, suddenly which is to get something done quickly without warning and the other is earthquake. Every foundation of your trouble and predicament will be shaken to their core by your praise and worship and immediately all the doors holding you back will be opened at once and every band will be loosed in Jesus name, Amen.

> *"And brought them out, and said, Sirs, what must I do to be saved? And they said, Believe on the Lord Jesus Christ, and thou shalt be saved, and thy house." (Acts 16:30, 31)*

Your testimony will lead many to the Lord! Expect great

things happening from now on. Remember to give God all the glory.

Food for thought:

> *"Praise waiteth for thee, O God, in Zion: and unto thee shall the vow be performed." (Psalms 65:1)*

All New Testament believers dwell in Zion, so let us give Him praise and worship, and watch him do amazing things for us and all that pertains to us.

In heaven, praise is done on a consistent and regular basis. No wonder there is no chaos in heaven, no terrorist attack, no pestilence, no sickness and people do not die—because worship and praise is offered in heaven endlessly! So if the will of God will be done on the earth as it is in heaven, then we must replicate what exactly happens in heaven.

> *"And the four beasts had each of them six wings about him; and they were full of eyes within: and they rest not day and night, saying, Holy, holy, holy, Lord God Almighty, which was, and is, and is to come. And when those beasts give glory and honour and thanks to him that sat on the throne, who liveth for ever and ever, The four and twenty elders fall down before him that sat on the throne, and worship him that liveth for ever and ever, and cast their crowns before the throne, saying, Thou art worthy, O Lord, to receive glory and honour and power: for thou hast created all things, and for thy pleasure they are and were created." (Revelation 4:8-11)*

> *"And when he had taken the book, the four beasts and four and twenty elders fell down before the Lamb, having every one of them harps, and golden vials full of*

odours, which are the prayers of saints. And the four beasts said, Amen. And the four and twenty elders fell down and worshipped him that liveth for ever and ever." (Revelation 5:8, 14)

"And the four and twenty elders, which sat before God on their seats, fell upon their faces, and worshipped God, Saying, We give thee thanks, O Lord God Almighty, which art, and wast, and art to come; because thou hast taken to thee thy great power, and hast reigned." (Revelation 11:16, 17)

"And after these things I heard a great voice of much people in heaven, saying, Alleluia; Salvation, and glory, and honour, and power, unto the Lord our God: And again they said, Alleluia. And her smoke rose up for ever and ever. And the four and twenty elders and the four beasts fell down and worshipped God that sat on the throne, saying, Amen; Alleluia. And a voice came out of the throne, saying, Praise our God, all ye his servants, and ye that fear him, both small and great. And I heard as it were the voice of a great multitude, and as the voice of many waters, and as the voice of mighty thunderings, saying, Alleluia: for the Lord God omnipotent reigneth." (Revelation 19:1, 3-6)

There is something common with all these Bible verses listed above, we see that the twenty and four elders are constantly falling and worshipping our God. And 24 is a significant number; God does not just throw numbers around. We know the significance of 3, 5, 7, 10, 21, 40 and 50.

Likewise 24 is significant with respect to the number of hours in a day. God wants to be praised round the clock!

Even though none of us could praise and worship God for 24 hours none stop, but could it be that when 24 of us get together for 1 hour, we would have successfully produced one whole day of praise and worship? Imagine for a moment if we can even duplicate that! No wonder the Bible says

> *"But, beloved, be not ignorant of this one thing, that one day is with the Lord as a thousand years, and a thousand years as one day." (2 Peter 3:8)*

Here's my thought, and I will pose it to you as a probable concept:

That, if we have 24 people together praising God for one hour, it will amount to 24 hours of worship (and this corroborates the scripture that says "one will chase a thousand and two shall put ten thousand to flight").

And if you think that one hour is too much to praise God, then ask yourself if you a true disciple. Even Jesus asked His inner caucus "...couldest not thou watch one hour?" (Mark 14:37) It surely takes longer to see a full movie.

Within that one hour period, you can sing hymns, sing some choruses, listen to gospel songs, read or recite the psalms, and praise and worship the Lord in the Holy Ghost. It's not a time to ask for anything but a period of pure praise and worship that will last through the hour.

Here is a tiny hint that God gave us in the Bible how we can replicate the heavenly praise and worship system:

"And I heard the number of them which were sealed: and there were sealed an hundred and forty and four thousands of all the tribes of the children of Israel." (Revelation 7:4)

If we divide 144,000 by 24 it will give us 6000 units, as if to say that God Himself formed 6000 units of 24 elders from the tribe of Israel to praise Him.

Here is an idea that God gave me in 2015. We are starting CLUB 24E, which is going to be a mighty army of praisers and worshippers. And God has instructed me on how to connect the entire world, and this is what God is talking about here:

> *"After this I beheld, and, lo, a great multitude, which no man could number, of all nations, and kindreds, and people, and tongues, stood before the throne, and before the Lamb, clothed with white robes, and palms in their hands; And cried with a loud voice, saying, Salvation to our God which sitteth upon the throne, and unto the Lamb. And all the angels stood round about the throne, and about the elders and the four beasts, and fell before the throne on their faces, and worshipped God, Saying, Amen: Blessing, and glory, and wisdom, and thanksgiving, and honour, and power, and might, be unto our God for ever and ever. Amen." (Revelation 7:9-12)*

Here is what one of the elders in heaven was asking John the beloved:

> *"And one of the elders answered, saying unto me, what are these which are arrayed in white robes? And whence came they? And I said unto him, Sir, thou knowest. And he said to me, these are they which came out of great tribulation, and have washed their robes, and made them white in the blood of the Lamb." (Revelation 7:13, 14)*

Have you washed your robe and made it white in the blood of the Lamb? Are you ready to be part of the end time praise and worship team that will usher in the presence of God that is sorely needed at this time? If so then you are qualified to join this club.

Food for thought:

> *"But, beloved, be not ignorant of this one thing, that one day is with the Lord as a thousand years, and a thousand years as one day." (2 Peter 3:8)*

> *"And I heard the number of them which were sealed: and there were sealed an hundred and forty and four thousands of all the tribes of the children of Israel. Of the tribe of Judah were sealed twelve thousand. Of the tribe of Reuben were sealed twelve thousand. Of the tribe of Gad were sealed twelve thousand. Of the tribe of Aser were sealed twelve thousand. Of the tribe of Nepthalim were sealed twelve thousand. Of the tribe of Manasses were sealed twelve thousand. Of the tribe of Simeon were sealed twelve thousand. Of the tribe of Levi were sealed twelve thousand. Of the tribe of Issachar were sealed twelve thousand. Of the tribe of Zabulon were sealed twelve thousand. Of the tribe of Joseph were sealed twelve thousand. Of the tribe of Benjamin were sealed twelve thousand. After this I beheld, and, lo, a great multitude, which no man could number, of all nations, and kindreds, and people, and tongues, stood before the throne, and before the Lamb, clothed with white robes, and palms in their hands; And cried with a loud voice, saying, Salvation to our God which sitteth upon the throne, and unto the Lamb. And all the angels stood round about the throne, and about the elders and*

the four beasts, and fell before the throne on their faces, and worshipped God, Saying, Amen: Blessing, and glory, and wisdom, and thanksgiving, and honour, and power, and might, be unto our God for ever and ever. Amen. And one of the elders answered, saying unto me, what are these which are arrayed in white robes? And whence came they? And I said unto him, Sir, thou knowest. And he said to me, these are they which came out of great tribulation, and have washed their robes, and made them white in the blood of the Lamb. Therefore are they before the throne of God, and serve him day and night in his temple: and he that sitteth on the throne shall dwell among them. They shall hunger no more, neither thirst anymore; neither shall the sun light on them, nor any heat. For the Lamb which is in the midst of the throne shall feed them, and shall lead them unto living fountains of waters: and God shall wipe away all tears from their eyes." (Revelation 7:4-17)

ABOUT THE AUTHOR

Dr. Olalekan Joseph Olowe is a physical therapist by trade and a pastor by calling. Together with his wife, Omolade, they are the Presiding Servants over Kingdom Dominion Ministry International (KDMI) with a ministry base at El Paso, Texas from where they reach out globally.

A graduate of Rocky Mountain University of Health Professionals with a transitional Doctorate in Physical Therapy, Joseph is blessed with a physical therapy practice in El Paso, Texas.

He's a prolific writer and the author of I Am Three Dimensional, Living Free: The Power of Self-Control amongst other books. He's happily married to Omolade and they are blessed with three children.

KINGDOM DOMINION MINISTRY
INTERNATIONAL (KDMI)

To partner with us or to be part of Kingdom Dominion Ministry International (KDMI), please call or write us

1800-561-9170 or +1 915-478-8807

P. O Box 10499
El Paso, TX 79995

info@hisdominion.org | www.hisdominion.org